THE NATURE NOTEBOOK SERIES

EDITED BY
ANNA BOTSFORD COMSTOCK

THE FISH NOTEBOOK

BY
GEORGE C. EMBODY

ASSISTANT PROFESSOR OF AGRICULTURE
CORNELL UNIVERSITY

THE COMSTOCK PUBLISHING COMPANY
ITHACA, NEW YORK

THIS EDITION PUBLISHED 2021
BY
LIVING BOOK PRESS IN ASSOCIATION WITH HEARTHROOM PRESS

ORIGINAL WORK PUBLISHED 1915
BY
THE COMSTOCK PUBLISHING COMPANY

FOR MORE INFORMATION, CONTACT:
HEARTHROOM PRESS
INFO@HEARTHROOMPRESS.COM

ISBN: 978-1-922634-41-2

A catalogue record for this
book is available from the
National Library of Australia

THE purpose of this notebook is to show the way for the beginner in the study of fishes. It contains no keys for their identification, but may serve to prepare one for the use of those in larger works by pointing out some of the important structures which distinguishes the fishes, one from another. None the less, important is the consideration of fish habitats, and habits of feeding and of providing for their young. We know so little about them that even the beginner stands a good chance of contributing new facts. Notes relating to these topics may have practical value, for they will have to do with both fish economy and human economy. Some species are beneficial to man in one way or another , contributing food directly or indirectly, or keeping obnoxious aquatic organisms under control. Others are neutral, while still others are obnoxious in that they destroy the useful.

The stream, pond, or lake should be the first resort for securing specimens. The public aquarium and the fish market, however, must not be neglected, for the former will often have on exhibition rare and interesting forms, and the latter will usually be displaying many of the more important food fishes, the majority of which are difficult to secure in the field.

Among the utensils necessary for success in the field are the dipnet and a wide-mouthed bottle of fruit jar. A serviceable dipnet consists of a rather heavy iron ring fourteen to sixteen inches in diameter mounted in a long rake handle, the ring to be covered with course bobbinet. The depth of the net should be six inches or more greater than the diameter of the ring. one of the folding dipnets may be used but it will be found to be less rigid and consequently less serviceable when one is working in aquatic vegetation. The dipnet is especially useful in a small stream. It should be placed in the lower end of a pool and close to one bank. The current will keep the bag filled out. Another person with a long stout stick should now begin to poke into the bank and try to pry up stones, first well upstream and then gradually working down towards the net. The whole driving process should be continued with speed and when within two or three feet of the net, the latter should be taken up quickly. In a pond where vegetation is thick, many fishes may be taken by drawing the net quickly through it. The bottle or glass jar is used to facilitate observations upon small fishes. In the air a fish does not show its fins nor its coloration to advantage. If placed in a jar full of water, these features together with the fish movements may be more clearly observed without injuring the specimen.

More ambitious collectors may successfully use a minnow seine or minnow trap both of which will add materially to the catch in a large stream or pond. A seine should be selected which is not over twenty feet long and which has a good bag at the center. (Figure 1).

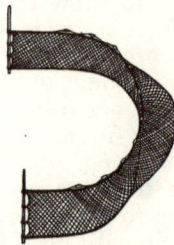

Fig. 1 – Minnow Seine   Fig. 2 – Home-made Minnow trap

A minnow trap me be purchased or may be made at home our of galvanized wire screen. (Figure 2). The trap should be baited by placing inside, a chunk of dry bread or salt pork. It is then tied to the end of a long stout cord or wire and tossed out into the pond. The free end of the cord is secured on shore.

Before attempting to fill the outlines on subsequent pages, one will have to familiarize himself with various external parts of a fish. The following figures are presented to assist in this procedure. It is suggested that all structures be recognized in a living fish by comparing same with figures 1 to 9. And finally it will help to fix these parts in mind, if one will make a drawing of one or more fishes from life and label clearly each part.

There are some things called for in the outlines which need explanation. The dorsal fin formula: if we count the rays in the dorsal fin of a sunfish, (figure 3), we find there are ten spines and twelve soft rays.

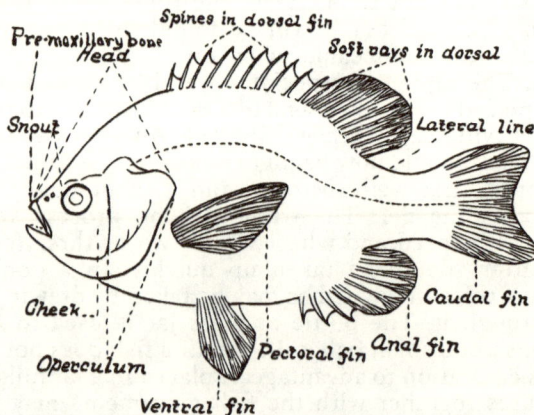

Fig. 3 - Sunfish wish terminal mouth, upward curved lateral line, ventral fins thoracic in position and compressed body.

4

It is customary to indicate the number of spines by Roman numerals and the number of soft rays by the Arabic and in writing the formula we separate the two by a comma. Thus the formula for the dorsal fin of a sunfish is, D. X, 12.

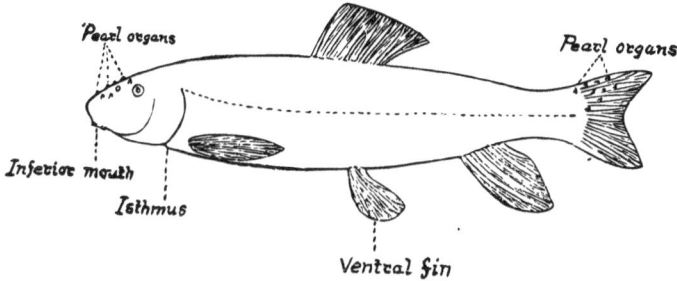

Fig. 4 - Sunfish wish terminal mouth, upward curved lateral line, ventral fins thoracic in position and compressed body.

When the dorsal is divided into a first and second, a formula for each is given and these are separated by a hyphen. This, D. XIII-II, 12 indicates thirteen spines in the first dorsal, and two spines and twelve soft rays in the second.

The adipose fin, (figure 5), since it has no supporting rays is not considered when determining the dorsal fin formula.

Some fishes have teeth and some, like the minnows, have none. If teeth are present, they are usually found on the edges of the jaws, in the roof of the mouth, and on the tongue. If studying a living fish, press the mouth open and carefully pass the blunt blade of a penknife over the roof of the mouth and the tongue. IF the sensation is like passing the knife blade over a file, the teeth are present.

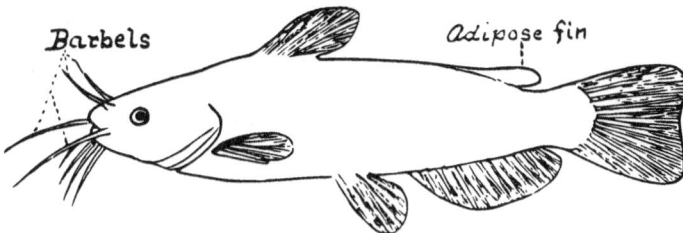

Fig. 5 - Bullhead with adipose fin (a mere flap of tissue without rays) and barbels.

The form of the body of a fish may be compressed or cylindrical. It is compressed when the depth of the fish is greater than its thickness, as in the sunfish and goldfish. It is cylindrical, when the depth equals the thickness.

The mouth of a fish may open directly to the front as in the sunfish which position is called terminal. When it opens directly downward, as in the sucker, it is called inferior. It is subterminal when opening diagonally downward, and subsuperior when opening diagonally upward. (See figs. 10 and 11, p.).

The premaxillary looks like the upper lip of the fish; (see fig 3). It is movable in some species and not in others. If it can be pulled forward with the fingers it is called movable, in which case a groove behind it is noticeable.

The ventral fins are sometimes situated directly under the pectorals they are abdominal in position. (See figs. 3 and 4, page 5).

In the latter half of this book will be found drawings of some fifty-four different kinds of fishes representing practically every fish water family. These have been redrawn largely from plates of Forbes and Richardson, Jordan and Evermann, and H.M. Smith; but a few are from photographs. They are intended not only to assist in naming a particular fish but to serve as a means for recording the colors and markings. Crayons or colored pencils may be taken afield and each figure colored from the living specimen.

It may be impracticable or impossible for many to obtain in the field all the required notes relating to the habits of fishes. When such is the case, it is suggested that one or more of the works mentioned on the next page, be consulted. It must be remembered, however, that complete accounts of the habits of American Fishes are few and widely scattered.

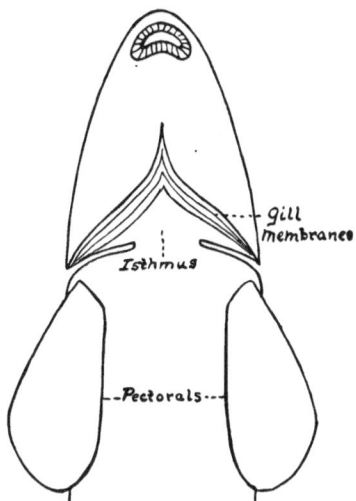

Fig. 6 - Ventral aspect of head and breast region of a sucker showing isthmus joined to gill membranes.

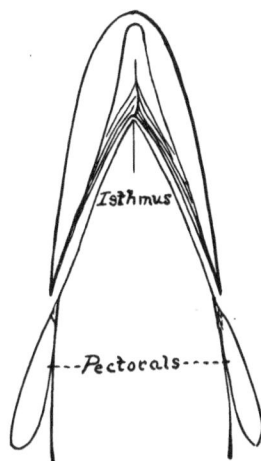

Fig. 7 - Ventral aspect of head and breast region of a sunfish showing isthmus not joined to gill mem-branes.

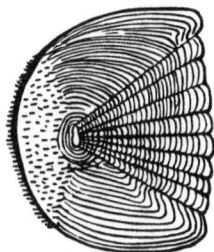

Fig. 8 - Ctenoid or rough scale of a sunfish. The minute spines on the right-hand side and margin distinguish this type of scale.

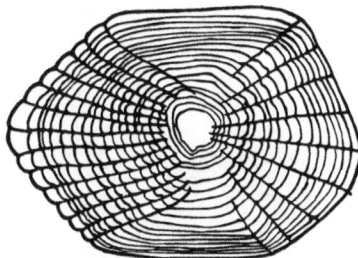

Fig. 9 - Cycloid or smooth scale of a sucker. Note absence of minute spines.

Fig. 10 - Subterminal mouth of black-nosed Dace.

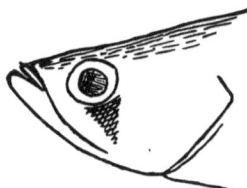

Fig. 11 - Subsuperior mouth of Killifish.

BOOKS ON FISHES
FOR FURTHER READING

A MANUAL OF VERTEBRATE ANIMALS OF THE NORTHERN
UNITED STATES. By David Starr Jordan. A.C. McClurg and Co.,
Publishers. Gives keys for the determination of species.

AMERICAN FOOD AND GAME FISHES. BY JORDAN AND
EVERMANN. DOUBLEDAY, PAGE & CO. Includes keys and good
accounts of the habits of food fishes.

A GUIDE TO THE STUDY OF FISHES. BY JORDAN. HENRY HOLT.

THE FISHES OF ILLINOIS. By Forbes and Richardson. Bulletin
Illinois State Laboratory. Gives keys and excellent accounts of the
distribution and food of many of our fresh water fishes. Numerous
half-tones and colored plates.

THE FISHES OF NORTH CAROLINA. BY HUGH M. SMITH.
Bulletin of the N.C. Geological Survey.

HANDBOOK OF NATURE STUDY. By A.B. Comstock. The
Comstock Pub Co. Pp. 149-180.

Male sunfish guarding his nest.

INDEX TO FISH NOTES

Name of Fish   Page

INDEX TO FISH NOTES

NAME OF FISH   PAGE

NOTES ON FISHES

Name of fish: Date:

See picture, page: Waters visited:

(Underscore the words applying to the particular species at hand)

Where seen: small brook, creek, river, pond, lake

1. Kind of water: cold spring, warm; clear or roily; rapids or pool; in vegetation or barren places

2. Kind of bottom: mud, sand, gravel or rocks

BODY. Form: compressed or cylindrical

HEAD.

    1.   Form: compressed, depressed, conical

    2.   Barbels or feelers: present, absent

    3.   Teeth: long and sharp, short and in pads, absent

    4.   Operculum: with or without scales

    5.   Cheek: with or without scales

    6.   Mouth: terminal, subterminal; sub-superior; inferior

    7.   Premaxillary bone: movable forward, or fixed

    8.   Gill membranes: free or joined to isthmus

FINS.

1. Dorsal: equal to or shorter than anal fin where joined to body; single, or partly or   wholly divided;

soft rays only or both spines and soft rays; dorsal fin formula.

2. Adipose fin: present or absent; free or joined to tail fin.

3. Caudal or tail fin; sketch its shape accurately:

4. Pectorals: armed with a spine or soft rays only

5. Ventrals or pelvics: abdominal or thoracic in position

LATERAL LINE: continuous, broken or absent; straight, curves upward or downward

SCALES: Large, medium, minute, wanting; smooth or rough, (to determine them, pass finger over side of body from tail towards head).

COLOR AND MARKINGS.

1. General ground color $\begin{cases} \text{back} \\ \text{sides} \\ \text{underparts} \end{cases}$

2. Longitudinal stripes $\begin{cases} \text{location} \\ \text{extent} \\ \text{color} \end{cases}$

3. Vertical bars $\begin{cases} \text{location} \\ \text{extent} \\ \text{color} \end{cases}$

4. Spots, blotches, mottlings, brilliant coloration.

Location and color:

SEX DIFFERENCES.

1. Pearl organs on male. Where?

2. Conspicuous colors and markings on male. Where?

FOOD consists of what?

EGGS. Where are they deposited?

Does this fish guard eggs and young?

MISCELLANEOUS.

Name of fish: Date:

See picture, page: Waters visited:

(Underscore the words applying to the particular species at hand)

Where seen: small brook, creek, river, pond, lake

1. Kind of water: cold spring, warm; clear or roily; rapids or pool; in vegetation or barren places

2. Kind of bottom: mud, sand, gravel or rocks

  BODY. Form: compressed or cylindrical

  HEAD.

    1.   Form: compressed, depressed, conical

    2.   Barbels or feelers: present, absent

    3.   Teeth: long and sharp, short and in pads, absent

    4.   Operculum: with or without scales

    5.   Cheek: with or without scales

    6.   Mouth: terminal, subterminal; sub-superior; inferior

    7.   Premaxillary bone: movable forward, or fixed

    8.   Gill membranes: free or joined to isthmus

  FINS.

    1. Dorsal: equal to or shorter than anal fin where joined to body; single, or partly or   wholly divided;

      soft rays only or both spines and soft rays; dorsal fin formula.

    2. Adipose fin: present or absent; free or joined to tail fin.

    3. Caudal or tail fin; sketch its shape accurately:

4. Pectorals: armed with a spine or soft rays only

5. Ventrals or pelvics: abdominal or thoracic in position

LATERAL LINE: continuous, broken or absent; straight, curves upward or downward

SCALES: Large, medium, minute, wanting; smooth or rough, (to determine them, pass finger over side of body from tail towards head).

COLOR AND MARKINGS.

1. General ground color $\begin{cases} \text{back} \\ \text{sides} \\ \text{underparts} \end{cases}$

2. Longitudinal stripes $\begin{cases} \text{location} \\ \text{extent} \\ \text{color} \end{cases}$

3. Vertical bars $\begin{cases} \text{location} \\ \text{extent} \\ \text{color} \end{cases}$

4. Spots, blotches, mottlings, brilliant coloration.

Location and color:

SEX DIFFERENCES.

1. Pearl organs on male. Where?

2. Conspicuous colors and markings on male. Where?

FOOD consists of what?

EGGS. Where are they deposited?

Does this fish guard eggs and young?

MISCELLANEOUS.

Name of fish: Date:

See picture, page: Waters visited:

(Underscore the words applying to the particular species at hand)

Where seen: small brook, creek, river, pond, lake

1. Kind of water: cold spring, warm; clear or roily; rapids or pool; in vegetation or barren places

2. Kind of bottom: mud, sand, gravel or rocks

BODY. Form: compressed or cylindrical

HEAD.

    1.   Form: compressed, depressed, conical

    2.   Barbels or feelers: present, absent

    3.   Teeth: long and sharp, short and in pads, absent

    4.   Operculum: with or without scales

    5.   Cheek: with or without scales

    6.   Mouth: terminal, subterminal; sub-superior; inferior

    7.   Premaxillary bone: movable forward, or fixed

    8.   Gill membranes: free or joined to isthmus

FINS.

1. Dorsal: equal to or shorter than anal fin where joined to body; single, or partly or   wholly divided;

soft rays only or both spines and soft rays; dorsal fin formula.

2. Adipose fin: present or absent; free or joined to tail fin.

3. Caudal or tail fin; sketch its shape accurately:

4. Pectorals: armed with a spine or soft rays only

5. Ventrals or pelvics: abdominal or thoracic in position

LATERAL LINE: continuous, broken or absent; straight, curves upward or downward

SCALES: Large, medium, minute, wanting; smooth or rough, (to determine them, pass finger over side of body from tail towards head).

COLOR AND MARKINGS.

1. General ground color $\begin{cases} \text{back} \\ \text{sides} \\ \text{underparts} \end{cases}$

2. Longitudinal stripes $\begin{cases} \text{location} \\ \text{extent} \\ \text{color} \end{cases}$

3. Vertical bars $\begin{cases} \text{location} \\ \text{extent} \\ \text{color} \end{cases}$

4. Spots, blotches, mottlings, brilliant coloration.

Location and color:

SEX DIFFERENCES.

1. Pearl organs on male. Where?

2. Conspicuous colors and markings on male. Where?

FOOD consists of what?

EGGS. Where are they deposited?

Does this fish guard eggs and young?

MISCELLANEOUS.

Name of fish: Date:

See picture, page: Waters visited:

(Underscore the words applying to the particular species at hand)

Where seen: small brook, creek, river, pond, lake

1. Kind of water: cold spring, warm; clear or roily; rapids or pool; in vegetation or barren places

2. Kind of bottom: mud, sand, gravel or rocks

BODY. Form: compressed or cylindrical

HEAD.

1.   Form: compressed, depressed, conical

2.   Barbels or feelers: present, absent

3.   Teeth: long and sharp, short and in pads, absent

4.   Operculum: with or without scales

5.   Cheek: with or without scales

6.   Mouth: terminal, subterminal; sub-superior; inferior

7.   Premaxillary bone: movable forward, or fixed

8.   Gill membranes: free or joined to isthmus

FINS.

1. Dorsal: equal to or shorter than anal fin where joined to body; single, or partly or   wholly divided;

   soft rays only or both spines and soft rays; dorsal fin formula.

2. Adipose fin: present or absent; free or joined to tail fin.

3. Caudal or tail fin; sketch its shape accurately:

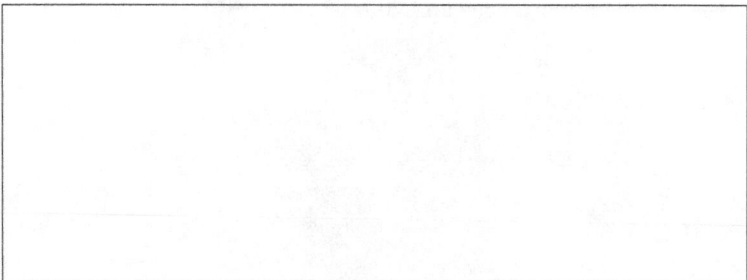

4. Pectorals: armed with a spine or soft rays only

5. Ventrals or pelvics: abdominal or thoracic in position

LATERAL LINE: continuous, broken or absent; straight, curves upward or downward

SCALES: Large, medium, minute, wanting; smooth or rough, (to determine them, pass finger over side of body from tail towards head).

COLOR AND MARKINGS.

1. General ground color $\begin{cases} \text{back} \\ \text{sides} \\ \text{underparts} \end{cases}$

2. Longitudinal stripes $\begin{cases} \text{location} \\ \text{extent} \\ \text{color} \end{cases}$

3. Vertical bars $\begin{cases} \text{location} \\ \text{extent} \\ \text{color} \end{cases}$

4. Spots, blotches, mottlings, brilliant coloration.

Location and color:

SEX DIFFERENCES.

1. Pearl organs on male. Where?

2. Conspicuous colors and markings on male. Where?

FOOD consists of what?

EGGS. Where are they deposited?

Does this fish guard eggs and young?

MISCELLANEOUS.

Name of fish: Date:

See picture, page: Waters visited:

(Underscore the words applying to the particular species at hand)

Where seen: small brook, creek, river, pond, lake

1. Kind of water: cold spring, warm; clear or roily; rapids or pool; in vegetation or barren places

2. Kind of bottom: mud, sand, gravel or rocks

  BODY. Form: compressed or cylindrical

  HEAD.

    1.   Form: compressed, depressed, conical

    2.   Barbels or feelers: present, absent

    3.   Teeth: long and sharp, short and in pads, absent

    4.   Operculum: with or without scales

    5.   Cheek: with or without scales

    6.   Mouth: terminal, subterminal; sub-superior; inferior

    7.   Premaxillary bone: movable forward, or fixed

    8.   Gill membranes: free or joined to isthmus

  FINS.

1. Dorsal: equal to or shorter than anal fin where joined to body; single, or partly or   wholly divided;

  soft rays only or both spines and soft rays; dorsal fin formula.

2. Adipose fin: present or absent; free or joined to tail fin.

3. Caudal or tail fin; sketch its shape accurately:

4. Pectorals: armed with a spine or soft rays only

5. Ventrals or pelvics: abdominal or thoracic in position

LATERAL LINE: continuous, broken or absent; straight, curves upward or downward

SCALES: Large, medium, minute, wanting; smooth or rough, (to determine them, pass finger over side of body from tail towards head).

COLOR AND MARKINGS.

1. General ground color $\begin{cases} \text{back} \\ \text{sides} \\ \text{underparts} \end{cases}$

2. Longitudinal stripes $\begin{cases} \text{location} \\ \text{extent} \\ \text{color} \end{cases}$

3. Vertical bars $\begin{cases} \text{location} \\ \text{extent} \\ \text{color} \end{cases}$

4. Spots, blotches, mottlings, brilliant coloration.

Location and color:

SEX DIFFERENCES.

1. Pearl organs on male. Where?

2. Conspicuous colors and markings on male. Where?

FOOD consists of what?

EGGS. Where are they deposited?

Does this fish guard eggs and young?

MISCELLANEOUS.

Name of fish: Date:

See picture, page: Waters visited:

(Underscore the words applying to the particular species at hand)

Where seen: small brook, creek, river, pond, lake

1. Kind of water: cold spring, warm; clear or roily; rapids or pool; in vegetation or barren places

2. Kind of bottom: mud, sand, gravel or rocks

BODY. Form: compressed or cylindrical

HEAD.

    1.   Form: compressed, depressed, conical

    2.   Barbels or feelers: present, absent

    3.   Teeth: long and sharp, short and in pads, absent

    4.   Operculum: with or without scales

    5.   Cheek: with or without scales

    6.   Mouth: terminal, subterminal; sub-superior; inferior

    7.   Premaxillary bone: movable forward, or fixed

    8.   Gill membranes: free or joined to isthmus

FINS.

1. Dorsal: equal to or shorter than anal fin where joined to body; single, or partly or   wholly divided;

    soft rays only or both spines and soft rays; dorsal fin formula.

2. Adipose fin: present or absent; free or joined to tail fin.

3. Caudal or tail fin; sketch its shape accurately:

4. Pectorals: armed with a spine or soft rays only

5. Ventrals or pelvics: abdominal or thoracic in position

LATERAL LINE: continuous, broken or absent; straight, curves upward or downward

SCALES: Large, medium, minute, wanting; smooth or rough, (to determine them, pass finger over side of body from tail towards head).

COLOR AND MARKINGS.

1. General ground color $\begin{cases} \text{back} \\ \text{sides} \\ \text{underparts} \end{cases}$

2. Longitudinal stripes $\begin{cases} \text{location} \\ \text{extent} \\ \text{color} \end{cases}$

3. Vertical bars $\begin{cases} \text{location} \\ \text{extent} \\ \text{color} \end{cases}$

4. Spots, blotches, mottlings, brilliant coloration.

Location and color:

SEX DIFFERENCES.

1. Pearl organs on male. Where?

2. Conspicuous colors and markings on male. Where?

FOOD consists of what?

EGGS. Where are they deposited?

Does this fish guard eggs and young?

MISCELLANEOUS.

Name of fish: Date:

See picture, page: Waters visited:

(Underscore the words applying to the particular species at hand)

Where seen: small brook, creek, river, pond, lake

1. Kind of water: cold spring, warm; clear or roily; rapids or pool; in vegetation or barren places

2. Kind of bottom: mud, sand, gravel or rocks

  BODY. Form: compressed or cylindrical

  HEAD.

> 1.   Form: compressed, depressed, conical
>
> 2.   Barbels or feelers: present, absent
>
> 3.   Teeth: long and sharp, short and in pads, absent
>
> 4.   Operculum: with or without scales
>
> 5.   Cheek: with or without scales
>
> 6.   Mouth: terminal, subterminal; sub-superior; inferior
>
> 7.   Premaxillary bone: movable forward, or fixed
>
> 8.   Gill membranes: free or joined to isthmus

  FINS.

1. Dorsal: equal to or shorter than anal fin where joined to body; single, or partly or   wholly divided;

   soft rays only or both spines and soft rays; dorsal fin formula.

2. Adipose fin: present or absent; free or joined to tail fin.

3. Caudal or tail fin; sketch its shape accurately:

4. Pectorals: armed with a spine or soft rays only

5. Ventrals or pelvics: abdominal or thoracic in position

LATERAL LINE: continuous, broken or absent; straight, curves upward or downward

SCALES: Large, medium, minute, wanting; smooth or rough, (to determine them, pass finger over side of body from tail towards head).

COLOR AND MARKINGS.

1. General ground color $\begin{cases} \text{back} \\ \text{sides} \\ \text{underparts} \end{cases}$

2. Longitudinal stripes $\begin{cases} \text{location} \\ \text{extent} \\ \text{color} \end{cases}$

3. Vertical bars $\begin{cases} \text{location} \\ \text{extent} \\ \text{color} \end{cases}$

4. Spots, blotches, mottlings, brilliant coloration.

Location and color:

SEX DIFFERENCES.

1. Pearl organs on male. Where?

2. Conspicuous colors and markings on male. Where?

FOOD consists of what?

EGGS. Where are they deposited?

Does this fish guard eggs and young?

MISCELLANEOUS.

Name of fish: Date:

See picture, page: Waters visited:

(Underscore the words applying to the particular species at hand)

Where seen: small brook, creek, river, pond, lake

1. Kind of water: cold spring, warm; clear or roily; rapids or pool; in vegetation or barren places

2. Kind of bottom: mud, sand, gravel or rocks

BODY. Form: compressed or cylindrical

HEAD.

1.	Form: compressed, depressed, conical
2.	Barbels or feelers: present, absent
3.	Teeth: long and sharp, short and in pads, absent
4.	Operculum: with or without scales
5.	Cheek: with or without scales
6.	Mouth: terminal, subterminal; sub-superior; inferior
7.	Premaxillary bone: movable forward, or fixed
8.	Gill membranes: free or joined to isthmus

FINS.

1. Dorsal: equal to or shorter than anal fin where joined to body; single, or partly or   wholly divided;

soft rays only or both spines and soft rays; dorsal fin formula.

2. Adipose fin: present or absent; free or joined to tail fin.

3. Caudal or tail fin; sketch its shape accurately:

4. Pectorals: armed with a spine or soft rays only

5. Ventrals or pelvics: abdominal or thoracic in position

LATERAL LINE: continuous, broken or absent; straight, curves upward or downward

SCALES: Large, medium, minute, wanting; smooth or rough, (to determine them, pass finger over side of body from tail towards head).

COLOR AND MARKINGS.

1. General ground color $\begin{cases} \text{back} \\ \text{sides} \\ \text{underparts} \end{cases}$

2. Longitudinal stripes $\begin{cases} \text{location} \\ \text{extent} \\ \text{color} \end{cases}$

3. Vertical bars $\begin{cases} \text{location} \\ \text{extent} \\ \text{color} \end{cases}$

4. Spots, blotches, mottlings, brilliant coloration.

Location and color:

SEX DIFFERENCES.

1. Pearl organs on male. Where?

2. Conspicuous colors and markings on male. Where?

FOOD consists of what?

EGGS. Where are they deposited?

Does this fish guard eggs and young?

MISCELLANEOUS.

Name of fish: Date:

See picture, page: Waters visited:

(Underscore the words applying to the particular species at hand)

Where seen: small brook, creek, river, pond, lake

1. Kind of water: cold spring, warm; clear or roily; rapids or pool; in vegetation or barren places

2. Kind of bottom: mud, sand, gravel or rocks

BODY. Form: compressed or cylindrical

HEAD.

1.   Form: compressed, depressed, conical

2.   Barbels or feelers: present, absent

3.   Teeth: long and sharp, short and in pads, absent

4.   Operculum: with or without scales

5.   Cheek: with or without scales

6.   Mouth: terminal, subterminal; sub-superior; inferior

7.   Premaxillary bone: movable forward, or fixed

8.   Gill membranes: free or joined to isthmus

FINS.

1. Dorsal: equal to or shorter than anal fin where joined to body; single, or partly or   wholly divided;

soft rays only or both spines and soft rays; dorsal fin formula.

2. Adipose fin: present or absent; free or joined to tail fin.

3. Caudal or tail fin; sketch its shape accurately:

4. Pectorals: armed with a spine or soft rays only

5. Ventrals or pelvics: abdominal or thoracic in position

LATERAL LINE: continuous, broken or absent; straight, curves upward or downward

SCALES: Large, medium, minute, wanting; smooth or rough, (to determine them, pass finger over side of body from tail towards head).

COLOR AND MARKINGS.

1. General ground color $\begin{cases} \text{back} \\ \text{sides} \\ \text{underparts} \end{cases}$

2. Longitudinal stripes $\begin{cases} \text{location} \\ \text{extent} \\ \text{color} \end{cases}$

3. Vertical bars $\begin{cases} \text{location} \\ \text{extent} \\ \text{color} \end{cases}$

4. Spots, blotches, mottlings, brilliant coloration.

Location and color:

SEX DIFFERENCES.

1. Pearl organs on male. Where?

2. Conspicuous colors and markings on male. Where?

FOOD consists of what?

EGGS. Where are they deposited?

Does this fish guard eggs and young?

MISCELLANEOUS.

Name of fish: Date:

See picture, page: Waters visited:

(Underscore the words applying to the particular species at hand)

Where seen: small brook, creek, river, pond, lake

1. Kind of water: cold spring, warm; clear or roily; rapids or pool; in vegetation or barren places

2. Kind of bottom: mud, sand, gravel or rocks

BODY. Form: compressed or cylindrical

HEAD.

    1.   Form: compressed, depressed, conical

    2.   Barbels or feelers: present, absent

    3.   Teeth: long and sharp, short and in pads, absent

    4.   Operculum: with or without scales

    5.   Cheek: with or without scales

    6.   Mouth: terminal, subterminal; sub-superior; inferior

    7.   Premaxillary bone: movable forward, or fixed

    8.   Gill membranes: free or joined to isthmus

FINS.

1. Dorsal: equal to or shorter than anal fin where joined to body; single, or partly or   wholly divided;

  soft rays only or both spines and soft rays; dorsal fin formula.

2. Adipose fin: present or absent; free or joined to tail fin.

3. Caudal or tail fin; sketch its shape accurately:

4. Pectorals: armed with a spine or soft rays only

5. Ventrals or pelvics: abdominal or thoracic in position

LATERAL LINE: continuous, broken or absent; straight, curves upward or downward

SCALES: Large, medium, minute, wanting; smooth or rough, (to determine them, pass finger over side of body from tail towards head).

COLOR AND MARKINGS.

1. General ground color $\begin{cases} \text{back} \\ \text{sides} \\ \text{underparts} \end{cases}$

2. Longitudinal stripes $\begin{cases} \text{location} \\ \text{extent} \\ \text{color} \end{cases}$

3. Vertical bars $\begin{cases} \text{location} \\ \text{extent} \\ \text{color} \end{cases}$

4. Spots, blotches, mottlings, brilliant coloration.

Location and color:

SEX DIFFERENCES.

1. Pearl organs on male. Where?

2. Conspicuous colors and markings on male. Where?

FOOD consists of what?

EGGS. Where are they deposited?

Does this fish guard eggs and young?

MISCELLANEOUS.

Name of fish: Date:

See picture, page: Waters visited:

(Underscore the words applying to the particular species at hand)

Where seen: small brook, creek, river, pond, lake

1. Kind of water: cold spring, warm; clear or roily; rapids or pool; in vegetation or barren places

2. Kind of bottom: mud, sand, gravel or rocks

BODY. Form: compressed or cylindrical

HEAD.

1.	Form: compressed, depressed, conical
2.	Barbels or feelers: present, absent
3.	Teeth: long and sharp, short and in pads, absent
4.	Operculum: with or without scales
5.	Cheek: with or without scales
6.	Mouth: terminal, subterminal; sub-superior; inferior
7.	Premaxillary bone: movable forward, or fixed
8.	Gill membranes: free or joined to isthmus

FINS.

1. Dorsal: equal to or shorter than anal fin where joined to body; single, or partly or   wholly divided;

soft rays only or both spines and soft rays; dorsal fin formula.

2. Adipose fin: present or absent; free or joined to tail fin.

3. Caudal or tail fin; sketch its shape accurately:

4. Pectorals: armed with a spine or soft rays only

5. Ventrals or pelvics: abdominal or thoracic in position

LATERAL LINE: continuous, broken or absent; straight, curves upward or downward

SCALES: Large, medium, minute, wanting; smooth or rough, (to determine them, pass finger over side of body from tail towards head).

COLOR AND MARKINGS.

1. General ground color $\begin{cases} \text{back} \\ \text{sides} \\ \text{underparts} \end{cases}$

2. Longitudinal stripes $\begin{cases} \text{location} \\ \text{extent} \\ \text{color} \end{cases}$

3. Vertical bars $\begin{cases} \text{location} \\ \text{extent} \\ \text{color} \end{cases}$

4. Spots, blotches, mottlings, brilliant coloration.

Location and color:

SEX DIFFERENCES.

1. Pearl organs on male. Where?

2. Conspicuous colors and markings on male. Where?

FOOD consists of what?

EGGS. Where are they deposited?

Does this fish guard eggs and young?

MISCELLANEOUS.

Name of fish: Date:

See picture, page: Waters visited:

(Underscore the words applying to the particular species at hand)

Where seen: small brook, creek, river, pond, lake

1. Kind of water: cold spring, warm; clear or roily; rapids or pool; in vegetation or barren places

2. Kind of bottom: mud, sand, gravel or rocks

BODY. Form: compressed or cylindrical

HEAD.

    1.   Form: compressed, depressed, conical

    2.   Barbels or feelers: present, absent

    3.   Teeth: long and sharp, short and in pads, absent

    4.   Operculum: with or without scales

    5.   Cheek: with or without scales

    6.   Mouth: terminal, subterminal; sub-superior; inferior

    7.   Premaxillary bone: movable forward, or fixed

    8.   Gill membranes: free or joined to isthmus

FINS.

1. Dorsal: equal to or shorter than anal fin where joined to body; single, or partly or   wholly divided;

soft rays only or both spines and soft rays; dorsal fin formula.

2. Adipose fin: present or absent; free or joined to tail fin.

3. Caudal or tail fin; sketch its shape accurately:

4. Pectorals: armed with a spine or soft rays only

5. Ventrals or pelvics: abdominal or thoracic in position

LATERAL LINE: continuous, broken or absent; straight, curves upward or downward

SCALES: Large, medium, minute, wanting; smooth or rough, (to determine them, pass finger over side of body from tail towards head).

COLOR AND MARKINGS.

1. General ground color $\begin{cases} \text{back} \\ \text{sides} \\ \text{underparts} \end{cases}$

2. Longitudinal stripes $\begin{cases} \text{location} \\ \text{extent} \\ \text{color} \end{cases}$

3. Vertical bars $\begin{cases} \text{location} \\ \text{extent} \\ \text{color} \end{cases}$

4. Spots, blotches, mottlings, brilliant coloration.

Location and color:

SEX DIFFERENCES.

1. Pearl organs on male. Where?

2. Conspicuous colors and markings on male. Where?

FOOD consists of what?

EGGS. Where are they deposited?

Does this fish guard eggs and young?

MISCELLANEOUS.

Name of fish: Date:

See picture, page: Waters visited:

(Underscore the words applying to the particular species at hand)

Where seen: small brook, creek, river, pond, lake

1. Kind of water: cold spring, warm; clear or roily; rapids or pool; in vegetation or barren places

2. Kind of bottom: mud, sand, gravel or rocks

BODY. Form: compressed or cylindrical

HEAD.

   1.   Form: compressed, depressed, conical

   2.   Barbels or feelers: present, absent

   3.   Teeth: long and sharp, short and in pads, absent

   4.   Operculum: with or without scales

   5.   Cheek: with or without scales

   6.   Mouth: terminal, subterminal; sub-superior; inferior

   7.   Premaxillary bone: movable forward, or fixed

   8.   Gill membranes: free or joined to isthmus

FINS.

   1. Dorsal: equal to or shorter than anal fin where joined to body; single, or partly or   wholly divided;

   soft rays only or both spines and soft rays; dorsal fin formula.

   2. Adipose fin: present or absent; free or joined to tail fin.

   3. Caudal or tail fin; sketch its shape accurately:

4. Pectorals: armed with a spine or soft rays only

5. Ventrals or pelvics: abdominal or thoracic in position

LATERAL LINE: continuous, broken or absent; straight, curves upward or downward

SCALES: Large, medium, minute, wanting; smooth or rough, (to determine them, pass finger over side of body from tail towards head).

COLOR AND MARKINGS.

1. General ground color $\begin{cases}\text{back} \\ \text{sides} \\ \text{underparts}\end{cases}$

2. Longitudinal stripes $\begin{cases}\text{location} \\ \text{extent} \\ \text{color}\end{cases}$

3. Vertical bars $\begin{cases}\text{location} \\ \text{extent} \\ \text{color}\end{cases}$

4. Spots, blotches, mottlings, brilliant coloration.

Location and color:

SEX DIFFERENCES.

1. Pearl organs on male. Where?

2. Conspicuous colors and markings on male. Where?

FOOD consists of what?

EGGS. Where are they deposited?

Does this fish guard eggs and young?

MISCELLANEOUS.

Name of fish: Date:

See picture, page: Waters visited:

(Underscore the words applying to the particular species at hand)

Where seen: small brook, creek, river, pond, lake

1. Kind of water: cold spring, warm; clear or roily; rapids or pool; in vegetation or barren places

2. Kind of bottom: mud, sand, gravel or rocks

BODY. Form: compressed or cylindrical

HEAD.

    1.   Form: compressed, depressed, conical

    2.   Barbels or feelers: present, absent

    3.   Teeth: long and sharp, short and in pads, absent

    4.   Operculum: with or without scales

    5.   Cheek: with or without scales

    6.   Mouth: terminal, subterminal; sub-superior; inferior

    7.   Premaxillary bone: movable forward, or fixed

    8.   Gill membranes: free or joined to isthmus

FINS.

1. Dorsal: equal to or shorter than anal fin where joined to body; single, or partly or   wholly divided;

soft rays only or both spines and soft rays; dorsal fin formula.

2. Adipose fin: present or absent; free or joined to tail fin.

3. Caudal or tail fin; sketch its shape accurately:

4. Pectorals: armed with a spine or soft rays only

5. Ventrals or pelvics: abdominal or thoracic in position

LATERAL LINE: continuous, broken or absent; straight, curves upward or downward

SCALES: Large, medium, minute, wanting; smooth or rough, (to determine them, pass finger over side of body from tail towards head).

COLOR AND MARKINGS.

1. General ground color $\begin{cases} \text{back} \\ \text{sides} \\ \text{underparts} \end{cases}$

2. Longitudinal stripes $\begin{cases} \text{location} \\ \text{extent} \\ \text{color} \end{cases}$

3. Vertical bars $\begin{cases} \text{location} \\ \text{extent} \\ \text{color} \end{cases}$

4. Spots, blotches, mottlings, brilliant coloration.

Location and color:

SEX DIFFERENCES.

1. Pearl organs on male. Where?

2. Conspicuous colors and markings on male. Where?

FOOD consists of what?

EGGS. Where are they deposited?

Does this fish guard eggs and young?

MISCELLANEOUS.

Name of fish: Date:

See picture, page: Waters visited:

(Underscore the words applying to the particular species at hand)

Where seen: small brook, creek, river, pond, lake

1. Kind of water: cold spring, warm; clear or roily; rapids or pool; in vegetation or barren places

2. Kind of bottom: mud, sand, gravel or rocks

BODY. Form: compressed or cylindrical

HEAD.

1.   Form: compressed, depressed, conical

2.   Barbels or feelers: present, absent

3.   Teeth: long and sharp, short and in pads, absent

4.   Operculum: with or without scales

5.   Cheek: with or without scales

6.   Mouth: terminal, subterminal; sub-superior; inferior

7.   Premaxillary bone: movable forward, or fixed

8.   Gill membranes: free or joined to isthmus

FINS.

1. Dorsal: equal to or shorter than anal fin where joined to body; single, or partly or   wholly divided;

soft rays only or both spines and soft rays; dorsal fin formula.

2. Adipose fin: present or absent; free or joined to tail fin.

3. Caudal or tail fin; sketch its shape accurately:

4. Pectorals: armed with a spine or soft rays only

5. Ventrals or pelvics: abdominal or thoracic in position

LATERAL LINE: continuous, broken or absent; straight, curves upward or downward

SCALES: Large, medium, minute, wanting; smooth or rough, (to determine them, pass finger over side of body from tail towards head).

COLOR AND MARKINGS.

1. General ground color $\begin{cases} \text{back} \\ \text{sides} \\ \text{underparts} \end{cases}$

2. Longitudinal stripes $\begin{cases} \text{location} \\ \text{extent} \\ \text{color} \end{cases}$

3. Vertical bars $\begin{cases} \text{location} \\ \text{extent} \\ \text{color} \end{cases}$

4. Spots, blotches, mottlings, brilliant coloration.

Location and color:

SEX DIFFERENCES.

1. Pearl organs on male. Where?

2. Conspicuous colors and markings on male. Where?

FOOD consists of what?

EGGS. Where are they deposited?

Does this fish guard eggs and young?

MISCELLANEOUS.

Name of fish: Date:

See picture, page: Waters visited:

(Underscore the words applying to the particular species at hand)

Where seen: small brook, creek, river, pond, lake

1. Kind of water: cold spring, warm; clear or roily; rapids or pool; in vegetation or barren places

2. Kind of bottom: mud, sand, gravel or rocks

BODY. Form: compressed or cylindrical

HEAD.

1.	Form: compressed, depressed, conical
2.	Barbels or feelers: present, absent
3.	Teeth: long and sharp, short and in pads, absent
4.	Operculum: with or without scales
5.	Cheek: with or without scales
6.	Mouth: terminal, subterminal; sub-superior; inferior
7.	Premaxillary bone: movable forward, or fixed
8.	Gill membranes: free or joined to isthmus

FINS.

1. Dorsal: equal to or shorter than anal fin where joined to body; single, or partly or   wholly divided;

soft rays only or both spines and soft rays; dorsal fin formula.

2. Adipose fin: present or absent; free or joined to tail fin.

3. Caudal or tail fin; sketch its shape accurately:

4. Pectorals: armed with a spine or soft rays only

5. Ventrals or pelvics: abdominal or thoracic in position

LATERAL LINE: continuous, broken or absent; straight, curves upward or downward

SCALES: Large, medium, minute, wanting; smooth or rough, (to determine them, pass finger over side of body from tail towards head).

COLOR AND MARKINGS.

1. General ground color $\begin{cases} \text{back} \\ \text{sides} \\ \text{underparts} \end{cases}$

2. Longitudinal stripes $\begin{cases} \text{location} \\ \text{extent} \\ \text{color} \end{cases}$

3. Vertical bars $\begin{cases} \text{location} \\ \text{extent} \\ \text{color} \end{cases}$

4. Spots, blotches, mottlings, brilliant coloration.

Location and color:

SEX DIFFERENCES.

1. Pearl organs on male. Where?

2. Conspicuous colors and markings on male. Where?

FOOD consists of what?

EGGS. Where are they deposited?

Does this fish guard eggs and young?

MISCELLANEOUS.

Name of fish: Date:

See picture, page: Waters visited:

(Underscore the words applying to the particular species at hand)

Where seen: small brook, creek, river, pond, lake

1. Kind of water: cold spring, warm; clear or roily; rapids or pool; in vegetation or barren places

2. Kind of bottom: mud, sand, gravel or rocks

BODY. Form: compressed or cylindrical

HEAD.

   1.   Form: compressed, depressed, conical

   2.   Barbels or feelers: present, absent

   3.   Teeth: long and sharp, short and in pads, absent

   4.   Operculum: with or without scales

   5.   Cheek: with or without scales

   6.   Mouth: terminal, subterminal; sub-superior; inferior

   7.   Premaxillary bone: movable forward, or fixed

   8.   Gill membranes: free or joined to isthmus

FINS.

   1. Dorsal: equal to or shorter than anal fin where joined to body; single, or partly or   wholly divided;

   soft rays only or both spines and soft rays; dorsal fin formula.

   2. Adipose fin: present or absent; free or joined to tail fin.

   3. Caudal or tail fin; sketch its shape accurately:

4. Pectorals: armed with a spine or soft rays only

5. Ventrals or pelvics: abdominal or thoracic in position

LATERAL LINE: continuous, broken or absent; straight, curves upward or downward

SCALES: Large, medium, minute, wanting; smooth or rough, (to determine them, pass finger over side of body from tail towards head).

COLOR AND MARKINGS.

1. General ground color $\begin{cases} \text{back} \\ \text{sides} \\ \text{underparts} \end{cases}$

2. Longitudinal stripes $\begin{cases} \text{location} \\ \text{extent} \\ \text{color} \end{cases}$

3. Vertical bars $\begin{cases} \text{location} \\ \text{extent} \\ \text{color} \end{cases}$

4. Spots, blotches, mottlings, brilliant coloration.

Location and color:

SEX DIFFERENCES.

1. Pearl organs on male. Where?

2. Conspicuous colors and markings on male. Where?

FOOD consists of what?

EGGS. Where are they deposited?

Does this fish guard eggs and young?

MISCELLANEOUS.

Name of fish: Date:

See picture, page: Waters visited:

(Underscore the words applying to the particular species at hand)

Where seen: small brook, creek, river, pond, lake

1. Kind of water: cold spring, warm; clear or roily; rapids or pool; in vegetation or barren places

2. Kind of bottom: mud, sand, gravel or rocks

BODY. Form: compressed or cylindrical

HEAD.

    1.   Form: compressed, depressed, conical

    2.   Barbels or feelers: present, absent

    3.   Teeth: long and sharp, short and in pads, absent

    4.   Operculum: with or without scales

    5.   Cheek: with or without scales

    6.   Mouth: terminal, subterminal; sub-superior; inferior

    7.   Premaxillary bone: movable forward, or fixed

    8.   Gill membranes: free or joined to isthmus

FINS.

    1. Dorsal: equal to or shorter than anal fin where joined to body; single, or partly or   wholly divided;

    soft rays only or both spines and soft rays; dorsal fin formula.

    2. Adipose fin: present or absent; free or joined to tail fin.

    3. Caudal or tail fin; sketch its shape accurately:

4. Pectorals: armed with a spine or soft rays only

5. Ventrals or pelvics: abdominal or thoracic in position

LATERAL LINE: continuous, broken or absent; straight, curves upward or downward

SCALES: Large, medium, minute, wanting; smooth or rough, (to determine them, pass finger over side of body from tail towards head).

COLOR AND MARKINGS.

1. General ground color $\begin{cases} \text{back} \\ \text{sides} \\ \text{underparts} \end{cases}$

2. Longitudinal stripes $\begin{cases} \text{location} \\ \text{extent} \\ \text{color} \end{cases}$

3. Vertical bars $\begin{cases} \text{location} \\ \text{extent} \\ \text{color} \end{cases}$

4. Spots, blotches, mottlings, brilliant coloration.

Location and color:

SEX DIFFERENCES.

1. Pearl organs on male. Where?

2. Conspicuous colors and markings on male. Where?

FOOD consists of what?

EGGS. Where are they deposited?

Does this fish guard eggs and young?

MISCELLANEOUS.

Name of fish: Date:

See picture, page: Waters visited:

(Underscore the words applying to the particular species at hand)

Where seen: small brook, creek, river, pond, lake

1. Kind of water: cold spring, warm; clear or roily; rapids or pool; in vegetation or barren places

2. Kind of bottom: mud, sand, gravel or rocks

BODY. Form: compressed or cylindrical

HEAD.

   1.   Form: compressed, depressed, conical

   2.   Barbels or feelers: present, absent

   3.   Teeth: long and sharp, short and in pads, absent

   4.   Operculum: with or without scales

   5.   Cheek: with or without scales

   6.   Mouth: terminal, subterminal; sub-superior; inferior

   7.   Premaxillary bone: movable forward, or fixed

   8.   Gill membranes: free or joined to isthmus

FINS.

1. Dorsal: equal to or shorter than anal fin where joined to body; single, or partly or   wholly divided;

  soft rays only or both spines and soft rays; dorsal fin formula.

2. Adipose fin: present or absent; free or joined to tail fin.

3. Caudal or tail fin; sketch its shape accurately:

4. Pectorals: armed with a spine or soft rays only

5. Ventrals or pelvics: abdominal or thoracic in position

LATERAL LINE: continuous, broken or absent; straight, curves upward or downward

SCALES: Large, medium, minute, wanting; smooth or rough, (to determine them, pass finger over side of body from tail towards head).

COLOR AND MARKINGS.

1. General ground color $\begin{cases} \text{back} \\ \text{sides} \\ \text{underparts} \end{cases}$

2. Longitudinal stripes $\begin{cases} \text{location} \\ \text{extent} \\ \text{color} \end{cases}$

3. Vertical bars $\begin{cases} \text{location} \\ \text{extent} \\ \text{color} \end{cases}$

4. Spots, blotches, mottlings, brilliant coloration.

Location and color:

SEX DIFFERENCES.

1. Pearl organs on male. Where?

2. Conspicuous colors and markings on male. Where?

FOOD consists of what?

EGGS. Where are they deposited?

Does this fish guard eggs and young?

MISCELLANEOUS.

Name of fish: Date:

See picture, page: Waters visited:

(Underscore the words applying to the particular species at hand)

Where seen: small brook, creek, river, pond, lake

1. Kind of water: cold spring, warm; clear or roily; rapids or pool; in vegetation or barren places

2. Kind of bottom: mud, sand, gravel or rocks

 BODY. Form: compressed or cylindrical

 HEAD.

1.	Form: compressed, depressed, conical
2.	Barbels or feelers: present, absent
3.	Teeth: long and sharp, short and in pads, absent
4.	Operculum: with or without scales
5.	Cheek: with or without scales
6.	Mouth: terminal, subterminal; sub-superior; inferior
7.	Premaxillary bone: movable forward, or fixed
8.	Gill membranes: free or joined to isthmus

FINS.

1. Dorsal: equal to or shorter than anal fin where joined to body; single, or partly or   wholly divided;

soft rays only or both spines and soft rays; dorsal fin formula.

2. Adipose fin: present or absent; free or joined to tail fin.

3. Caudal or tail fin; sketch its shape accurately:

4. Pectorals: armed with a spine or soft rays only

5. Ventrals or pelvics: abdominal or thoracic in position

LATERAL LINE: continuous, broken or absent; straight, curves upward or downward

SCALES: Large, medium, minute, wanting; smooth or rough, (to determine them, pass finger over side of body from tail towards head).

COLOR AND MARKINGS.

1. General ground color $\begin{cases} \text{back} \\ \text{sides} \\ \text{underparts} \end{cases}$

2. Longitudinal stripes $\begin{cases} \text{location} \\ \text{extent} \\ \text{color} \end{cases}$

3. Vertical bars $\begin{cases} \text{location} \\ \text{extent} \\ \text{color} \end{cases}$

4. Spots, blotches, mottlings, brilliant coloration.

Location and color:

SEX DIFFERENCES.

1. Pearl organs on male. Where?

2. Conspicuous colors and markings on male. Where?

FOOD consists of what?

EGGS. Where are they deposited?

Does this fish guard eggs and young?

MISCELLANEOUS.

Name of fish: Date:

See picture, page: Waters visited:

(Underscore the words applying to the particular species at hand)

Where seen: small brook, creek, river, pond, lake

1. Kind of water: cold spring, warm; clear or roily; rapids or pool; in vegetation or barren places

2. Kind of bottom: mud, sand, gravel or rocks

BODY. Form: compressed or cylindrical

HEAD.

    1.   Form: compressed, depressed, conical

    2.   Barbels or feelers: present, absent

    3.   Teeth: long and sharp, short and in pads, absent

    4.   Operculum: with or without scales

    5.   Cheek: with or without scales

    6.   Mouth: terminal, subterminal; sub-superior; inferior

    7.   Premaxillary bone: movable forward, or fixed

    8.   Gill membranes: free or joined to isthmus

FINS.

  1. Dorsal: equal to or shorter than anal fin where joined to body; single, or partly or   wholly divided;

  soft rays only or both spines and soft rays; dorsal fin formula.

  2. Adipose fin: present or absent; free or joined to tail fin.

  3. Caudal or tail fin; sketch its shape accurately:

4. Pectorals: armed with a spine or soft rays only

5. Ventrals or pelvics: abdominal or thoracic in position

LATERAL LINE: continuous, broken or absent; straight, curves upward or downward

SCALES: Large, medium, minute, wanting; smooth or rough, (to determine them, pass finger over side of body from tail towards head).

COLOR AND MARKINGS.

1. General ground color $\begin{cases} \text{back} \\ \text{sides} \\ \text{underparts} \end{cases}$

2. Longitudinal stripes $\begin{cases} \text{location} \\ \text{extent} \\ \text{color} \end{cases}$

3. Vertical bars $\begin{cases} \text{location} \\ \text{extent} \\ \text{color} \end{cases}$

4. Spots, blotches, mottlings, brilliant coloration.

Location and color:

SEX DIFFERENCES.

1. Pearl organs on male. Where?

2. Conspicuous colors and markings on male. Where?

FOOD consists of what?

EGGS. Where are they deposited?

Does this fish guard eggs and young?

MISCELLANEOUS.

Name of fish: Date:

See picture, page: Waters visited:

(Underscore the words applying to the particular species at hand)

Where seen: small brook, creek, river, pond, lake

1. Kind of water: cold spring, warm; clear or roily; rapids or pool; in vegetation or barren places

2. Kind of bottom: mud, sand, gravel or rocks

BODY. Form: compressed or cylindrical

HEAD.

1.   Form: compressed, depressed, conical

2.   Barbels or feelers: present, absent

3.   Teeth: long and sharp, short and in pads, absent

4.   Operculum: with or without scales

5.   Cheek: with or without scales

6.   Mouth: terminal, subterminal; sub-superior; inferior

7.   Premaxillary bone: movable forward, or fixed

8.   Gill membranes: free or joined to isthmus

FINS.

1. Dorsal: equal to or shorter than anal fin where joined to body; single, or partly or   wholly divided;

   soft rays only or both spines and soft rays; dorsal fin formula.

2. Adipose fin: present or absent; free or joined to tail fin.

3. Caudal or tail fin; sketch its shape accurately:

4. Pectorals: armed with a spine or soft rays only

5. Ventrals or pelvics: abdominal or thoracic in position

LATERAL LINE: continuous, broken or absent; straight, curves upward or downward

SCALES: Large, medium, minute, wanting; smooth or rough, (to determine them, pass finger over side of body from tail towards head).

COLOR AND MARKINGS.

1. General ground color $\begin{cases} \text{back} \\ \text{sides} \\ \text{underparts} \end{cases}$

2. Longitudinal stripes $\begin{cases} \text{location} \\ \text{extent} \\ \text{color} \end{cases}$

3. Vertical bars $\begin{cases} \text{location} \\ \text{extent} \\ \text{color} \end{cases}$

4. Spots, blotches, mottlings, brilliant coloration.

Location and color:

SEX DIFFERENCES.

1. Pearl organs on male. Where?

2. Conspicuous colors and markings on male. Where?

FOOD consists of what?

EGGS. Where are they deposited?

Does this fish guard eggs and young?

MISCELLANEOUS.

Name of fish: Date:

See picture, page: Waters visited:

(Underscore the words applying to the particular species at hand)

Where seen: small brook, creek, river, pond, lake

1. Kind of water: cold spring, warm; clear or roily; rapids or pool; in vegetation or barren places

2. Kind of bottom: mud, sand, gravel or rocks

  BODY. Form: compressed or cylindrical

  HEAD.

    1.   Form: compressed, depressed, conical

    2.   Barbels or feelers: present, absent

    3.   Teeth: long and sharp, short and in pads, absent

    4.   Operculum: with or without scales

    5.   Cheek: with or without scales

    6.   Mouth: terminal, subterminal; sub-superior; inferior

    7.   Premaxillary bone: movable forward, or fixed

    8.   Gill membranes: free or joined to isthmus

  FINS.

1. Dorsal: equal to or shorter than anal fin where joined to body; single, or partly or   wholly divided;

  soft rays only or both spines and soft rays; dorsal fin formula.

2. Adipose fin: present or absent; free or joined to tail fin.

3. Caudal or tail fin; sketch its shape accurately:

4. Pectorals: armed with a spine or soft rays only

5. Ventrals or pelvics: abdominal or thoracic in position

LATERAL LINE: continuous, broken or absent; straight, curves upward or downward

SCALES: Large, medium, minute, wanting; smooth or rough, (to determine them, pass finger over side of body from tail towards head).

COLOR AND MARKINGS.

1. General ground color $\begin{cases} \text{back} \\ \text{sides} \\ \text{underparts} \end{cases}$

2. Longitudinal stripes $\begin{cases} \text{location} \\ \text{extent} \\ \text{color} \end{cases}$

3. Vertical bars $\begin{cases} \text{location} \\ \text{extent} \\ \text{color} \end{cases}$

4. Spots, blotches, mottlings, brilliant coloration.

Location and color:

SEX DIFFERENCES.

1. Pearl organs on male. Where?

2. Conspicuous colors and markings on male. Where?

FOOD consists of what?

EGGS. Where are they deposited?

Does this fish guard eggs and young?

MISCELLANEOUS.

Name of fish: Date:

See picture, page: Waters visited:

(Underscore the words applying to the particular species at hand)

Where seen: small brook, creek, river, pond, lake

1. Kind of water: cold spring, warm; clear or roily; rapids or pool; in vegetation or barren places

2. Kind of bottom: mud, sand, gravel or rocks

BODY. Form: compressed or cylindrical

HEAD.

1.	Form: compressed, depressed, conical	
2.	Barbels or feelers: present, absent	
3.	Teeth: long and sharp, short and in pads, absent	
4.	Operculum: with or without scales	
5.	Cheek: with or without scales	
6.	Mouth: terminal, subterminal; sub-superior; inferior	
7.	Premaxillary bone: movable forward, or fixed	
8.	Gill membranes: free or joined to isthmus	

FINS.

1. Dorsal: equal to or shorter than anal fin where joined to body; single, or partly or   wholly divided;

soft rays only or both spines and soft rays; dorsal fin formula.

2. Adipose fin: present or absent; free or joined to tail fin.

3. Caudal or tail fin; sketch its shape accurately:

4. Pectorals: armed with a spine or soft rays only

5. Ventrals or pelvics: abdominal or thoracic in position

LATERAL LINE: continuous, broken or absent; straight, curves upward or downward

SCALES: Large, medium, minute, wanting; smooth or rough, (to determine them, pass finger over side of body from tail towards head).

COLOR AND MARKINGS.

1. General ground color $\begin{cases} back \\ sides \\ underparts \end{cases}$

2. Longitudinal stripes $\begin{cases} location \\ extent \\ color \end{cases}$

3. Vertical bars $\begin{cases} location \\ extent \\ color \end{cases}$

4. Spots, blotches, mottlings, brilliant coloration.

Location and color:

SEX DIFFERENCES.

1. Pearl organs on male. Where?

2. Conspicuous colors and markings on male. Where?

FOOD consists of what?

EGGS. Where are they deposited?

Does this fish guard eggs and young?

MISCELLANEOUS.

Name of fish: Date:

See picture, page: Waters visited:

(Underscore the words applying to the particular species at hand)

Where seen: small brook, creek, river, pond, lake

1. Kind of water: cold spring, warm; clear or roily; rapids or pool; in vegetation or barren places

2. Kind of bottom: mud, sand, gravel or rocks

BODY. Form: compressed or cylindrical

HEAD.

1.   Form: compressed, depressed, conical

2.   Barbels or feelers: present, absent

3.   Teeth: long and sharp, short and in pads, absent

4.   Operculum: with or without scales

5.   Cheek: with or without scales

6.   Mouth: terminal, subterminal; sub-superior; inferior

7.   Premaxillary bone: movable forward, or fixed

8.   Gill membranes: free or joined to isthmus

FINS.

1. Dorsal: equal to or shorter than anal fin where joined to body; single, or partly or   wholly divided;

soft rays only or both spines and soft rays; dorsal fin formula.

2. Adipose fin: present or absent; free or joined to tail fin.

3. Caudal or tail fin; sketch its shape accurately:

4. Pectorals: armed with a spine or soft rays only

5. Ventrals or pelvics: abdominal or thoracic in position

LATERAL LINE: continuous, broken or absent; straight, curves upward or downward

SCALES: Large, medium, minute, wanting; smooth or rough, (to determine them, pass finger over side of body from tail towards head).

COLOR AND MARKINGS.

1. General ground color $\begin{cases} \text{back} \\ \text{sides} \\ \text{underparts} \end{cases}$

2. Longitudinal stripes $\begin{cases} \text{location} \\ \text{extent} \\ \text{color} \end{cases}$

3. Vertical bars $\begin{cases} \text{location} \\ \text{extent} \\ \text{color} \end{cases}$

4. Spots, blotches, mottlings, brilliant coloration.

Location and color:

SEX DIFFERENCES.

1. Pearl organs on male. Where?

2. Conspicuous colors and markings on male. Where?

FOOD consists of what?

EGGS. Where are they deposited?

Does this fish guard eggs and young?

MISCELLANEOUS.

Name of fish: Date:

See picture, page: Waters visited:

(Underscore the words applying to the particular species at hand)

Where seen: small brook, creek, river, pond, lake

1. Kind of water: cold spring, warm; clear or roily; rapids or pool; in vegetation or barren places

2. Kind of bottom: mud, sand, gravel or rocks

BODY. Form: compressed or cylindrical

HEAD.

    1.   Form: compressed, depressed, conical

    2.   Barbels or feelers: present, absent

    3.   Teeth: long and sharp, short and in pads, absent

    4.   Operculum: with or without scales

    5.   Cheek: with or without scales

    6.   Mouth: terminal, subterminal; sub-superior; inferior

    7.   Premaxillary bone: movable forward, or fixed

    8.   Gill membranes: free or joined to isthmus

FINS.

1. Dorsal: equal to or shorter than anal fin where joined to body; single, or partly or   wholly divided;

soft rays only or both spines and soft rays; dorsal fin formula.

2. Adipose fin: present or absent; free or joined to tail fin.

3. Caudal or tail fin; sketch its shape accurately:

4. Pectorals: armed with a spine or soft rays only

5. Ventrals or pelvics: abdominal or thoracic in position

LATERAL LINE: continuous, broken or absent; straight, curves upward or downward

SCALES: Large, medium, minute, wanting; smooth or rough, (to determine them, pass finger over side of body from tail towards head).

COLOR AND MARKINGS.

1. General ground color $\begin{cases} \text{back} \\ \text{sides} \\ \text{underparts} \end{cases}$

2. Longitudinal stripes $\begin{cases} \text{location} \\ \text{extent} \\ \text{color} \end{cases}$

3. Vertical bars $\begin{cases} \text{location} \\ \text{extent} \\ \text{color} \end{cases}$

4. Spots, blotches, mottlings, brilliant coloration.

Location and color:

SEX DIFFERENCES.

1. Pearl organs on male. Where?

2. Conspicuous colors and markings on male. Where?

FOOD consists of what?

EGGS. Where are they deposited?

Does this fish guard eggs and young?

MISCELLANEOUS.

Name of fish: Date:

See picture, page: Waters visited:

(Underscore the words applying to the particular species at hand)

Where seen: small brook, creek, river, pond, lake

1. Kind of water: cold spring, warm; clear or roily; rapids or pool; in vegetation or barren places

2. Kind of bottom: mud, sand, gravel or rocks

BODY. Form: compressed or cylindrical

HEAD.

    1.   Form: compressed, depressed, conical

    2.   Barbels or feelers: present, absent

    3.   Teeth: long and sharp, short and in pads, absent

    4.   Operculum: with or without scales

    5.   Cheek: with or without scales

    6.   Mouth: terminal, subterminal; sub-superior; inferior

    7.   Premaxillary bone: movable forward, or fixed

    8.   Gill membranes: free or joined to isthmus

FINS.

1. Dorsal: equal to or shorter than anal fin where joined to body; single, or partly or   wholly divided;

soft rays only or both spines and soft rays; dorsal fin formula.

2. Adipose fin: present or absent; free or joined to tail fin.

3. Caudal or tail fin; sketch its shape accurately:

4. Pectorals: armed with a spine or soft rays only

5. Ventrals or pelvics: abdominal or thoracic in position

LATERAL LINE: continuous, broken or absent; straight, curves upward or downward

SCALES: Large, medium, minute, wanting; smooth or rough, (to determine them, pass finger over side of body from tail towards head).

COLOR AND MARKINGS.

1. General ground color $\begin{cases} \text{back} \\ \text{sides} \\ \text{underparts} \end{cases}$

2. Longitudinal stripes $\begin{cases} \text{location} \\ \text{extent} \\ \text{color} \end{cases}$

3. Vertical bars $\begin{cases} \text{location} \\ \text{extent} \\ \text{color} \end{cases}$

4. Spots, blotches, mottlings, brilliant coloration.

Location and color:

SEX DIFFERENCES.

1. Pearl organs on male. Where?

2. Conspicuous colors and markings on male. Where?

FOOD consists of what?

EGGS. Where are they deposited?

Does this fish guard eggs and young?

MISCELLANEOUS.

Name of fish: Date:

See picture, page: Waters visited:

(Underscore the words applying to the particular species at hand)

Where seen: small brook, creek, river, pond, lake

1. Kind of water: cold spring, warm; clear or roily; rapids or pool; in vegetation or barren places

2. Kind of bottom: mud, sand, gravel or rocks

BODY. Form: compressed or cylindrical

HEAD.

    1.   Form: compressed, depressed, conical

    2.   Barbels or feelers: present, absent

    3.   Teeth: long and sharp, short and in pads, absent

    4.   Operculum: with or without scales

    5.   Cheek: with or without scales

    6.   Mouth: terminal, subterminal; sub-superior; inferior

    7.   Premaxillary bone: movable forward, or fixed

    8.   Gill membranes: free or joined to isthmus

FINS.

1. Dorsal: equal to or shorter than anal fin where joined to body; single, or partly or   wholly divided;

soft rays only or both spines and soft rays; dorsal fin formula.

2. Adipose fin: present or absent; free or joined to tail fin.

3. Caudal or tail fin; sketch its shape accurately:

4. Pectorals: armed with a spine or soft rays only

5. Ventrals or pelvics: abdominal or thoracic in position

LATERAL LINE: continuous, broken or absent; straight, curves upward or downward

SCALES: Large, medium, minute, wanting; smooth or rough, (to determine them, pass finger over side of body from tail towards head).

COLOR AND MARKINGS.

1. General ground color $\begin{cases} \text{back} \\ \text{sides} \\ \text{underparts} \end{cases}$

2. Longitudinal stripes $\begin{cases} \text{location} \\ \text{extent} \\ \text{color} \end{cases}$

3. Vertical bars $\begin{cases} \text{location} \\ \text{extent} \\ \text{color} \end{cases}$

4. Spots, blotches, mottlings, brilliant coloration.

Location and color:

SEX DIFFERENCES.

1. Pearl organs on male. Where?

2. Conspicuous colors and markings on male. Where?

FOOD consists of what?

EGGS. Where are they deposited?

Does this fish guard eggs and young?

MISCELLANEOUS.

Fishes

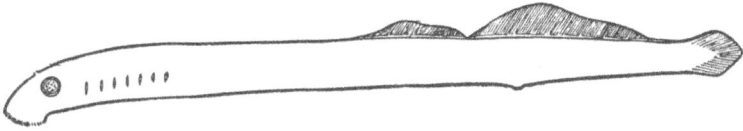

Lamprey, *Ichthyomyzon concolor*

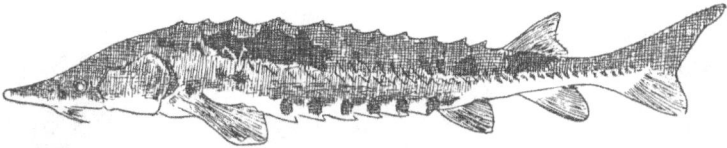

Lake Surgeon, *Acipenser rubicubdus*

Plate 1
*See Page*_____

Long-nosed Gar, *Lepisosteus osseus*

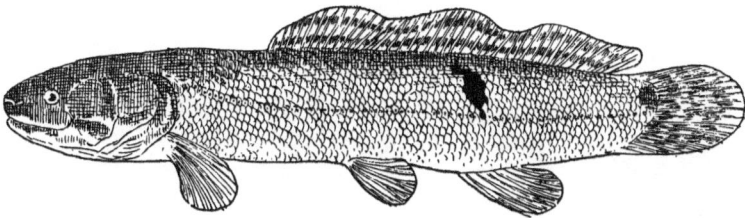

Dogfish or Bowfin, *Amia calva*

Plate 2
See Page _____

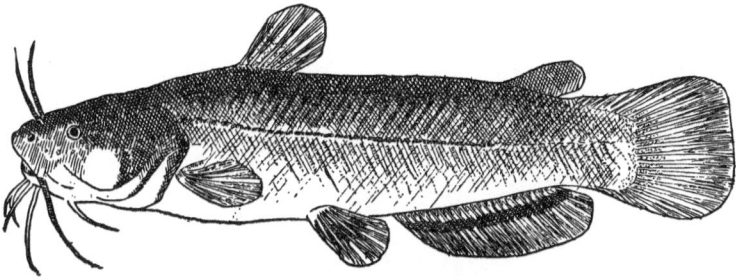

Common Bullhead, *Ameiurus nebulosus*

Plate 3
See Page _____

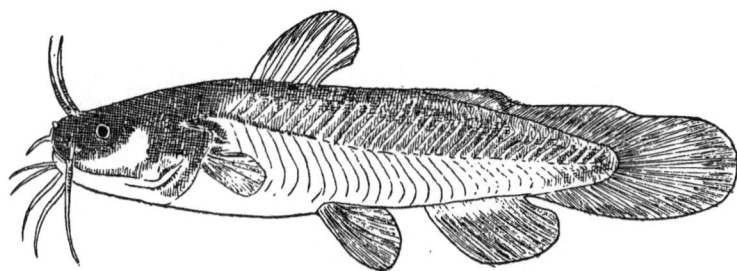

Tadpole Catfish, *Schilbeodes gyrinus*

Plate 4
See Page _____

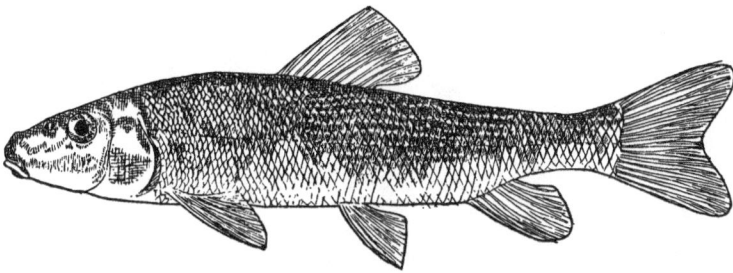

Sucker, *Catostomus commersonii*

Plate 5
See Page _____

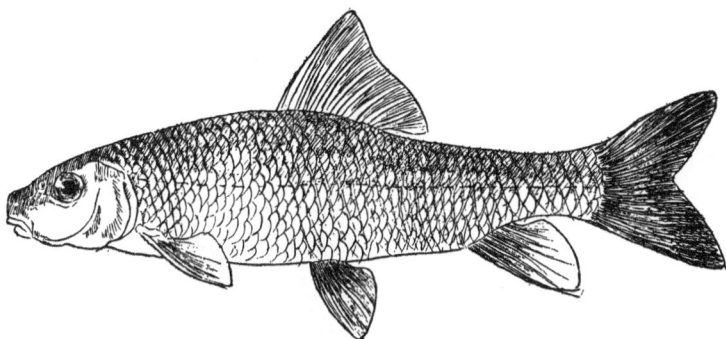

Red-horse Sucker, *Moxostoma breviceps*

Plate 6
See Page _____

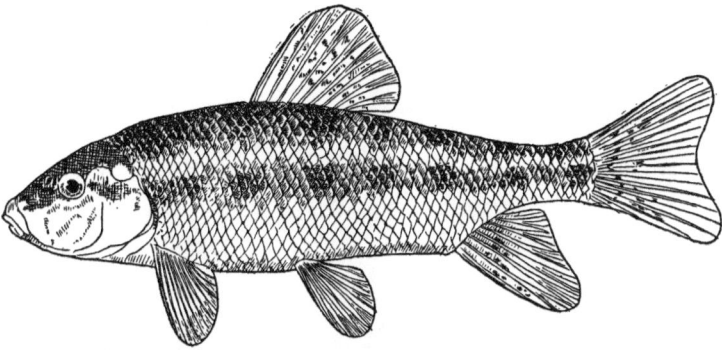

Chub-sucker, *Erimyzon sucetta*

Plate 7
See Page _____

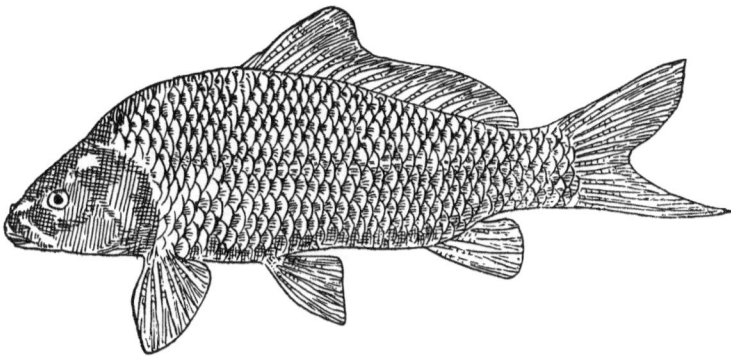

European Carp, *Cyprinus carpis*

Plate 8
See Page _____

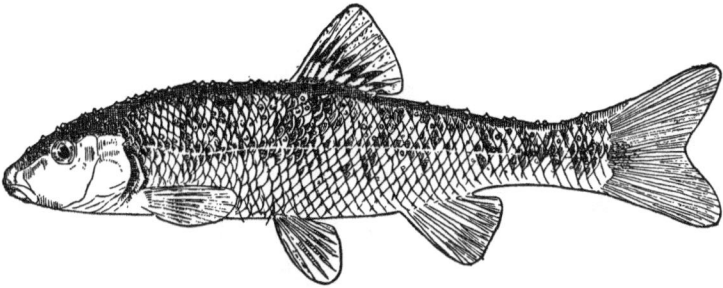

Stone Roller, *Campostima anomalun*

Plate 9
See Page _____

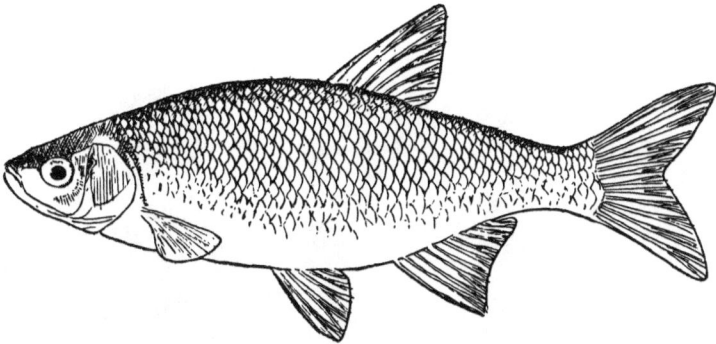

Golden Shiner, *Abramis crysolencas*

Plate 10
See Page _____

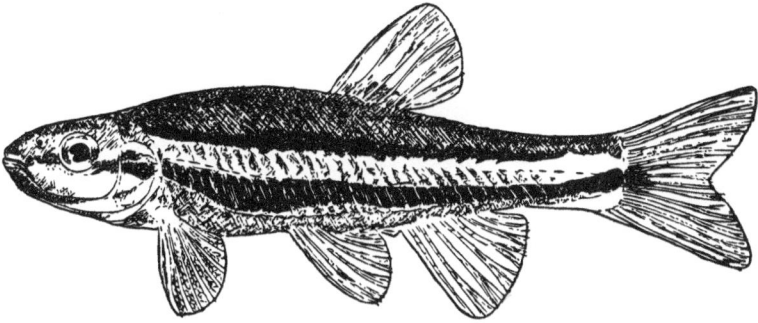

Red-bellied Dace, *Chrosomus erythrogaster*

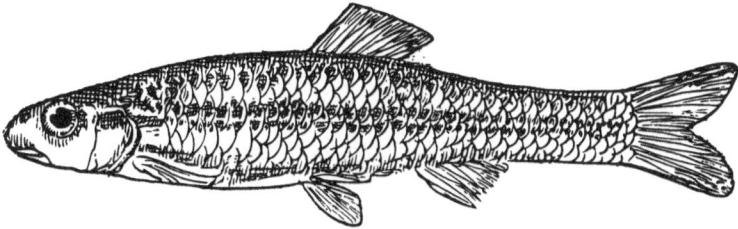

Blunt-nosed Minnow, *Pimephales notatus*

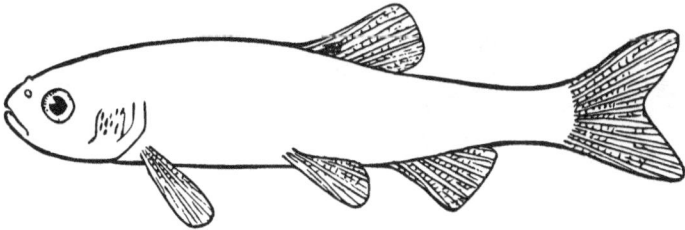

Horned Dace or Brook Chub, *Semotilus atromaculatus*

Plate 11
See Page _____

93

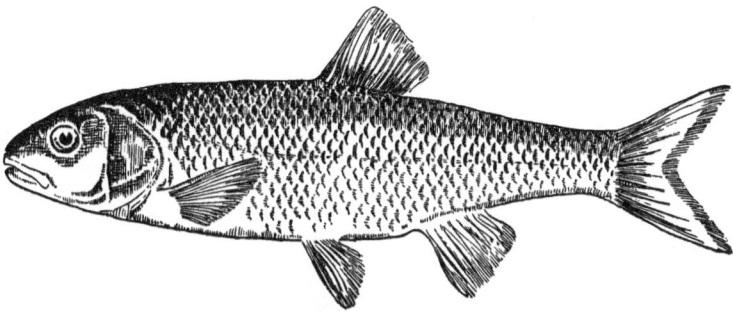

Fall Fish or River Chub, *Semotilus bullaris*

Plate 12
See Page _____

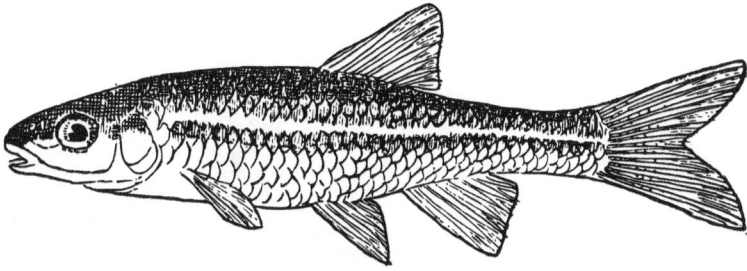

Cayuga Minnow, *Notropis cayuga*

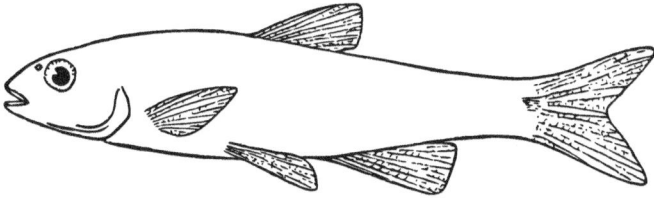

Spot-tailed Minnow, *Notropis hudsonius*

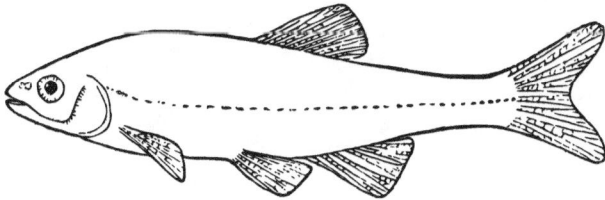

Satin-fin Shiner, *Notropis whipplei*

Plate 13
See Page _____

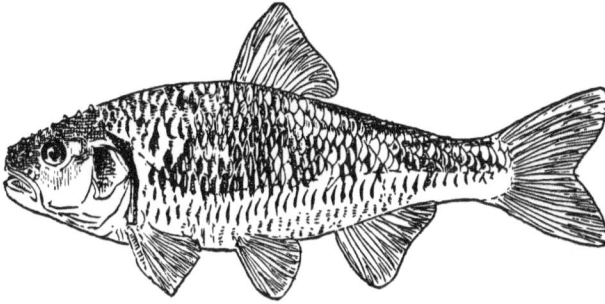

Common Red-fin Shiner, *Notropis cornutus*

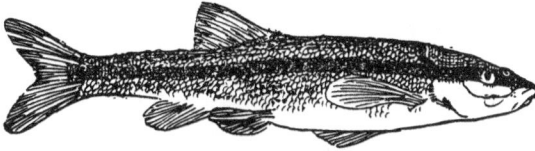

Black-nosed Dace, Rhinichthys atronasus

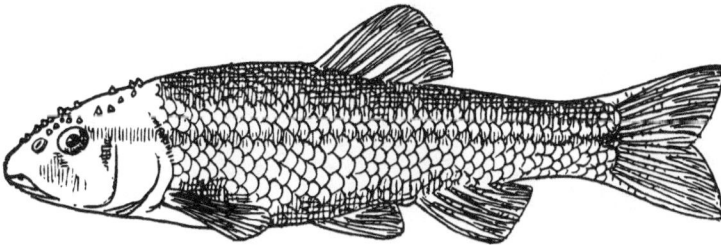

Horny-head Chub, Hybopsis kentuckiensis

Plate 14
See Page _____

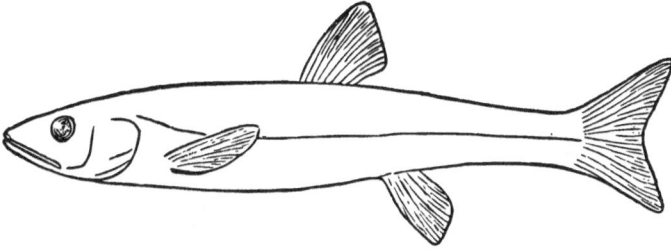

Red-sided Minnow, *Leuciscus elongatus*

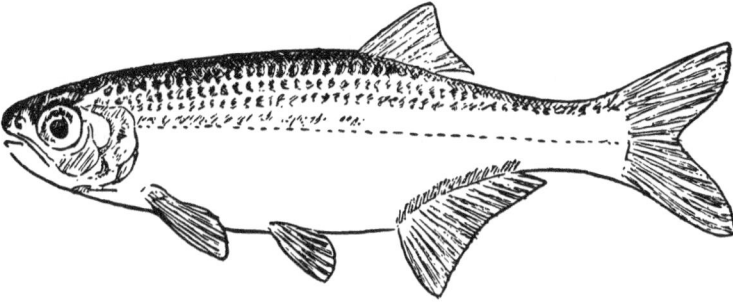

Toothed Herring, *Hyodon targisus*

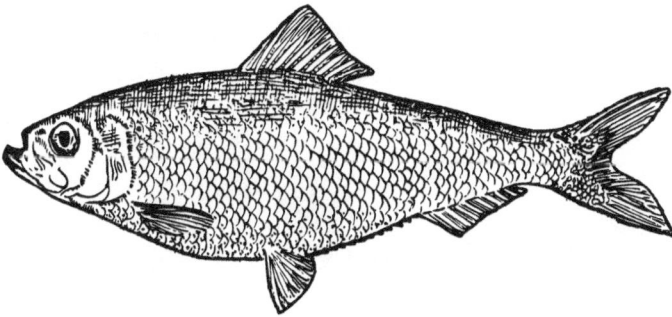

Alewife, Branch Herring, *Pomolobus pseudoharengus*

Plate 15
See Page _____

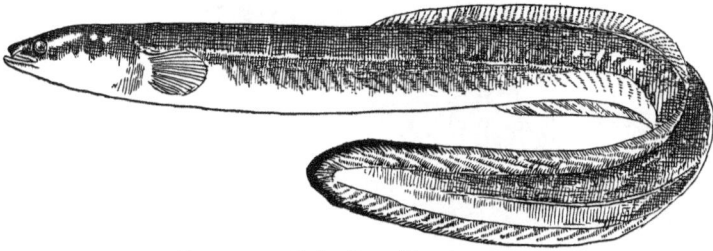

Common Eel, *Anguilla chrysypa*

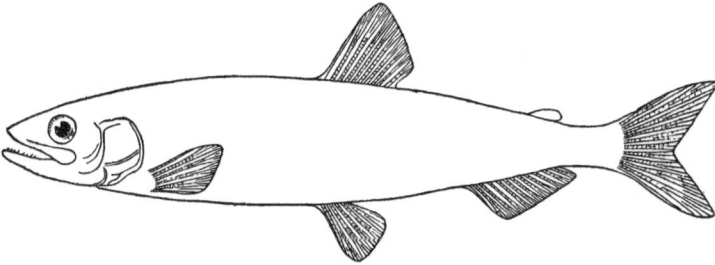

Smelt, *Osmerus mordax*

Plate 16
See Page _____

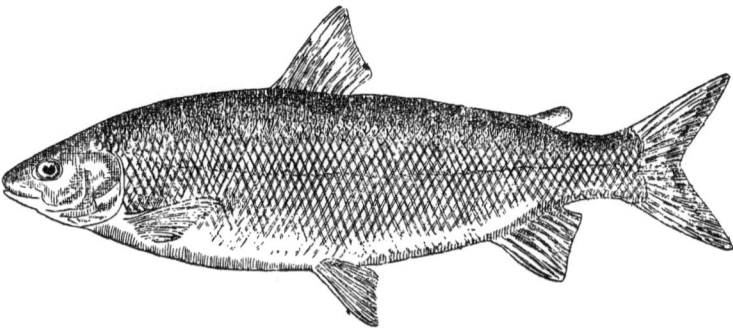

Whitefish, *Coregonus clupeiformis*

Plate 17
See Page _____

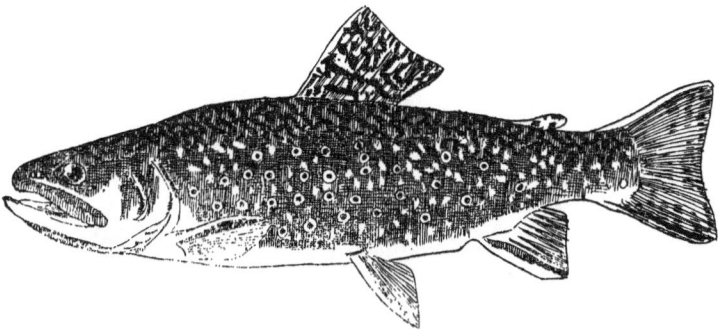

Brook Trout, *Salvelinus fontinalis*

Plate 18
See Page _____

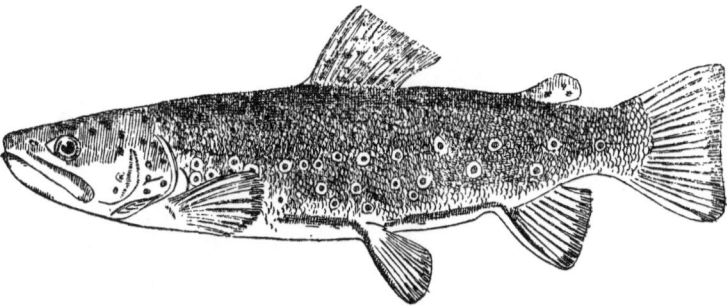

European Brook Trout or Brown Trout, *Salmo fario*

Plate 19
See Page _____

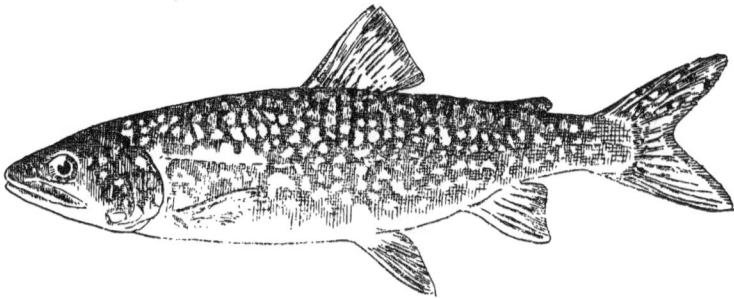

Lake Trout, *Cristivomer namaycush*

Plate 20
See Page _____

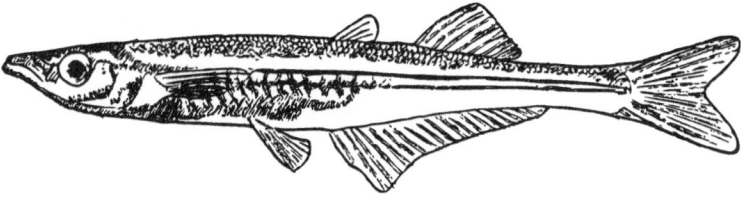

Brook Silversides, *Labidesthes sicculus*

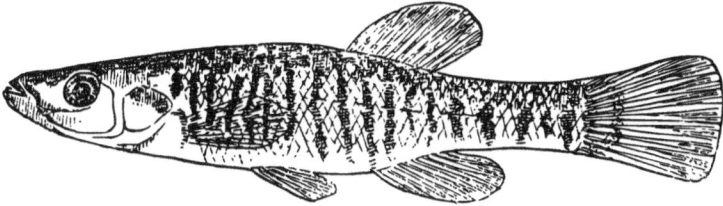

Fresh-water Killifish, *Fundulus diaphanus*

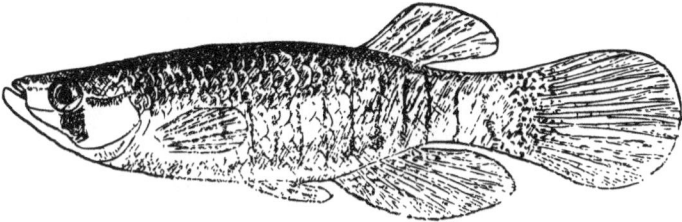

Top-minnow, *Fundulus dispar*

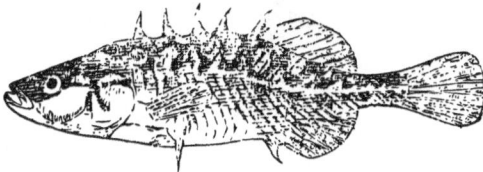

Brook Stickleback, *Eucalia inconstans*

Plate 21
See Page _____

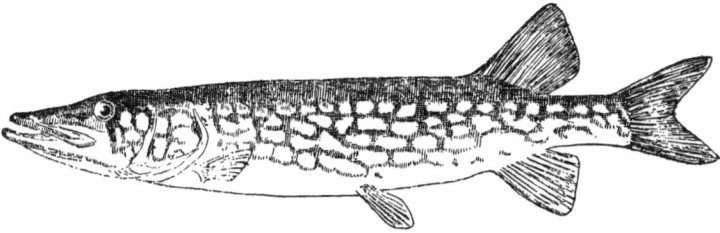

Reticulated Pickerel, *Esox reticulatus*

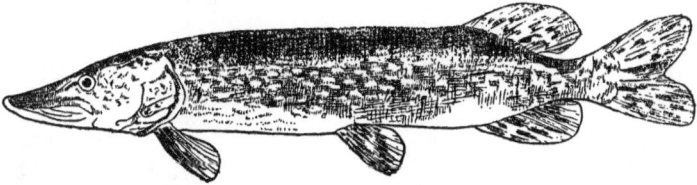

Common Pike, *Esox lucius*

Plate 22
See Page _____

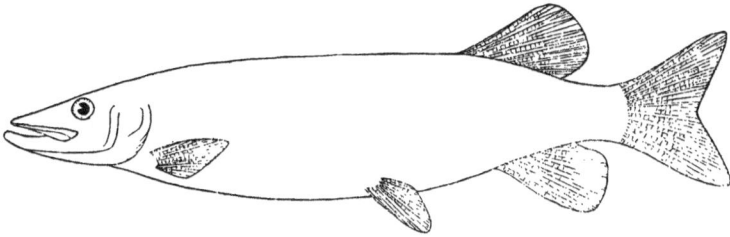

Mascalogne, *Esox masquinongy*

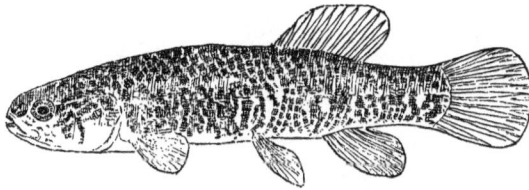

Mud-minnow, *Umbra limi*

Plate 23
See Page _____

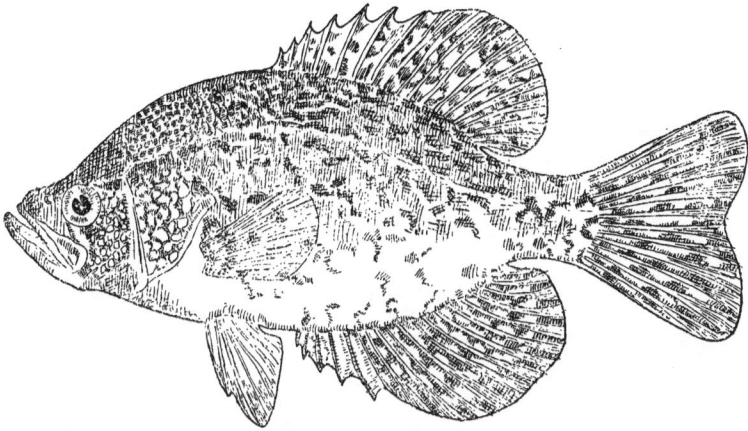

Calico Bass, *Pomoxis sparoides*

Plate 24
See Page _____

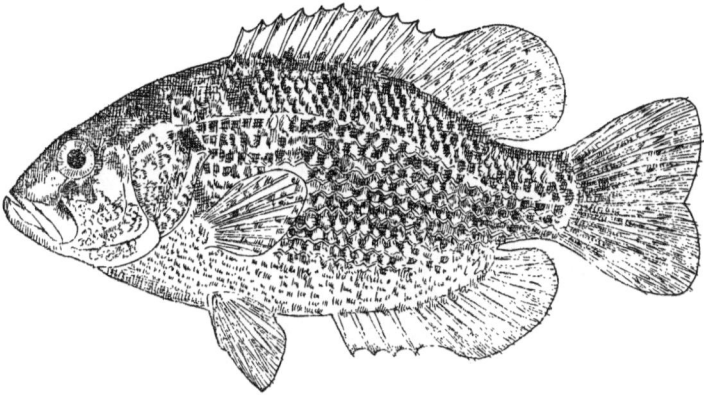

Rock Bass, *Ambloplites rupestris*

Plate 25
See Page _____

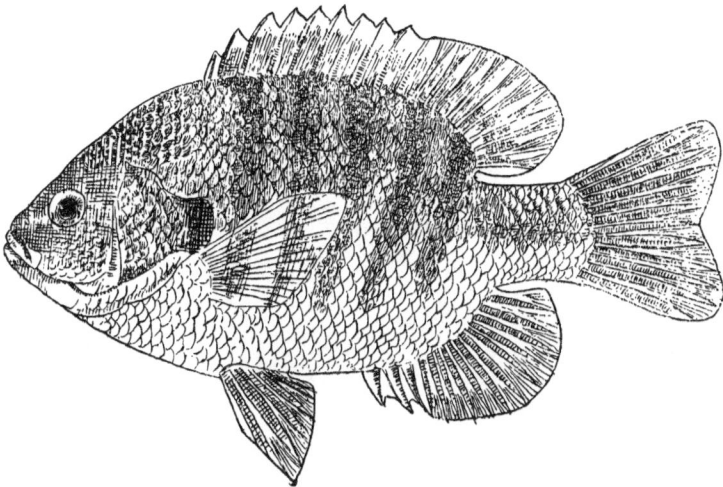

Bluegill Sunfish, *Lepomis pallidus*

Plate 26
See Page _____

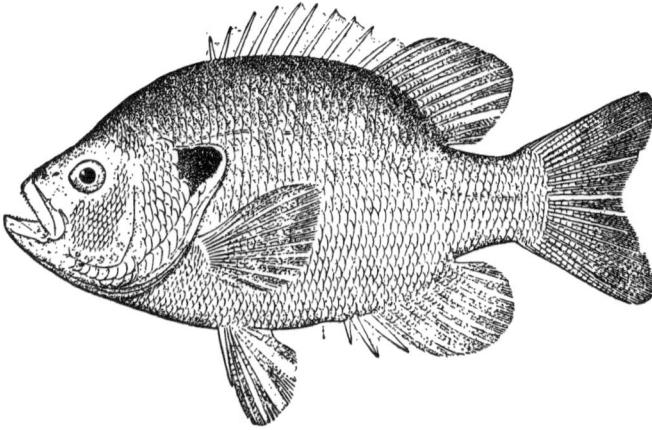

Common Sunfish, *Eupomotis gibbosus*

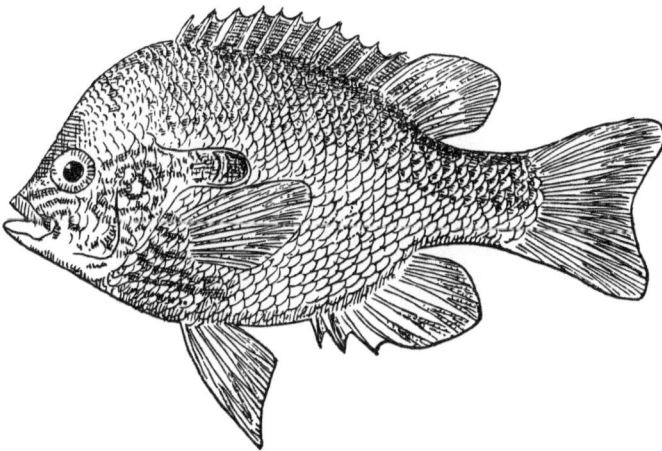

Long-eared Sunfish, *Lepomis megalotis*

Plate 27
See Page _____

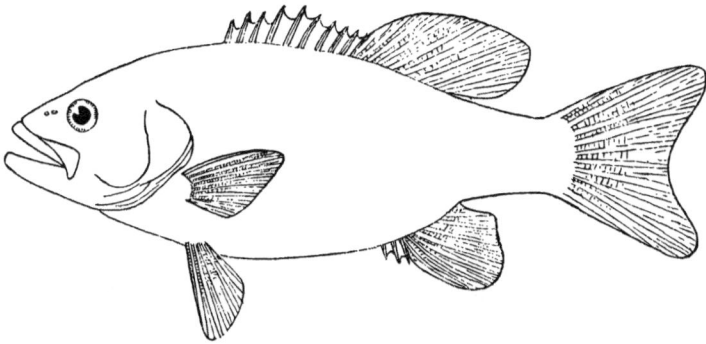

Small-mouthed Black Bass, *Micropterus dolomieu*

Plate 28
See Page _____

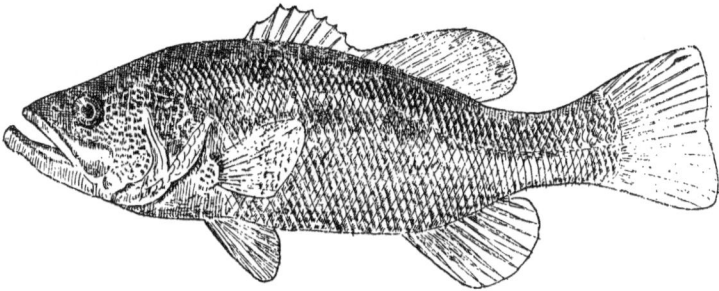

Large-mouthed Black Bass, *Micropterus salmoides*

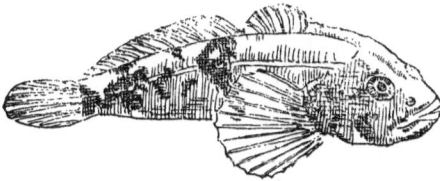

Common Sculpin or Blob, *Cottus ictalops*

Plate 29
See Page _____

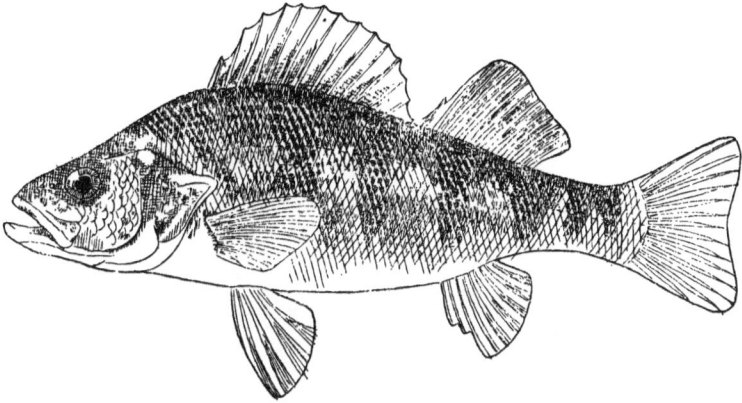

Yellow Perch, *Perca flavescens*

Plate 30
See Page _____

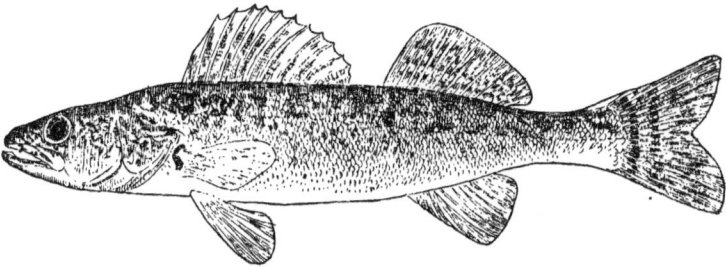

Pike Perch or Wall-eyed Pike, *Stizostedion vitreum*

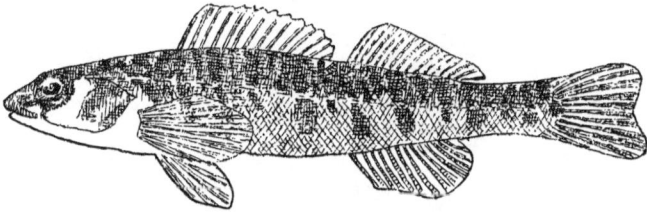

Log Perch, *Percina caprodes*

Plate 31
See Page _____

Johnny Darter, *Beleosoma nigrum*

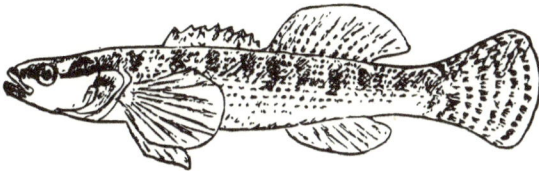

Fan-tailed Darter, *Etheostoma flabellare*

Rainbow Darter, *Etheostoma cœruleum*

Plate 32
See Page _____

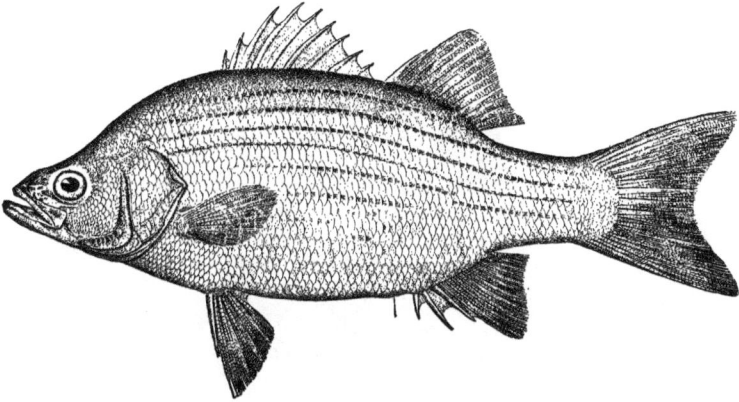

White Bass, *Roccus Chrysops*

Plate 33
See Page _____

Index   Plate   Page